FOOTBALL FOR FEMALES
The Women's Survival Guide to the Football Season

Teresa Saucedo-Artino

DORRANCE PUBLISHING CO, INC.
PITTSBURGH, PENNSYLVANIA 15222

ISBN # 978-0-8059-5108-0
Printed in the United States of America

Second Edition

For information or to order additional books, please write:
Dorrance Publishing Co., Inc.
701 Smithfield Street
Third Floor
Pittsburgh, Pennsylvania 15222
U.S.A.
1-800-788-7654
www.dorrancebookstore.com

To the men in my life: my husband and best friend Marc, and my three sons, Mike, Chris, and Rob. They encouraged me to watch football with them and then spent endless hours educating me, so I could enjoy the game as much as they do.

CONTENTS

INTRODUCTION

Do you think football is ridiculous? Are you tired of being a football widow? Are you tired of watching football without understanding the plays, the penalties, and the basic strategies of the game? Are you tired of being told, "You can only ask two questions" or have just given up because explanations you were given were so convoluted? And how about that entire male bonding stuff, high fives, belly bumping, and head butting?

Let's face it girlfriends, we may have sat through the games, but we certainly didn't understand them. In fact most of the time we didn't even watch but instead participated in meaningless chitchat or people-watched. We needed to find other ways to burn time, so we resorted to these senseless past times.

The thought of going through another football season watching a bunch of really big guys patting each other on the rear, head butting, wiggling on the field after a touchdown, or even hugging each other till they fall on or near that strangely shaped ball used to throw me into a state of depression.

That is until I started to understand the game. Football is actually an exciting game to watch and is easy to understand. After all if a male can understand the game, then no doubt the superior gender can also understand it. The problem is we haven't had the opportunity to learn it—until now. The time has come for all females to come to the aid of their senses and learn this seemingly silly game.

With the help of my husband and three sons, whose actual knowledge is legendary in their own minds, I shall attempt to cover the basics of football. Football is an intense and physical game, which is not played by sissies or mama's boys or watched by those weak of heart. In fact one of the reasons football is so popular with the hairier species is because it requires physical contact (not the good kind either) and a meathead mentality, thereby giving the male something to talk and boast about. Once you learn the game, you just may find yourself enjoying a game when no one else is around and quickly changing the channel when someone walks in the room.

After reading this book, I guarantee you will know more about football than the average potbellied, beer-drinking couch potato. In fact you will know enough to grow sprouts on those couch potatoes.

To grasp the concepts of this book, pop a beer, grab some beer nuts, plop yourself on the couch, and put your feet up on the coffee table. Two things you will not need are hairy armpits or a potbelly.

CHAPTER 1

TALK THE TALK, WALK THE WALK

Understanding the game of football requires a keen grasp of the football lingo. Remember you will be communicating with guys who will be using words, believe it or not, with more than four letters. After you learn the lingo you too will have a bounce in your step and glee in your eye with the mere mention of "football."

Following are the essentials you need along with an easy way to refresh your newly acquired football knowledge:

Armchair quarterback: A football "wannabe" coach or player. The wannabe will yell at the television, coach, or players: "reverse, reverse," "touchdown," "fumble," "pass interference," or "you're blind, ref." Like it makes a difference?

Astroturf: Fake grass used in the field of play. No matter how well it is maintained, just like zirconium it is still fake.

Backs: Not part of the human anatomy. They are the offensive players otherwise known as a fullback or halfback.

Backfield: The grassy area behind the line of scrimmage. Actually if the backfield didn't have those markings on the field it would be a nice place for a picnic.

Backward pass (lateral): A pass thrown parallel with or toward the passer's end line or to a player behind the passer.

Ball carrier: The big guy who has possession of the football.

Batting: This is not like baseball where the player bats the ball with a bat. Instead it means intentionally slapping or hitting the ball with an arm or hand.

Belly bumping: Extending the belly outward and toward one's opponent or own teammate. Actual touching must occur for it to be considered a true belly bump. No touchy, no bumpy.

Blackout: Temporary loss of consciousness due to a bump on the head or too much alcohol in the blood stream. But in football, it means the local game has not been sold out and the NFL will not allow the game to be broadcast on the local networks.

Blitz: A mad dash toward the quarterback by a cornerback or safety. A defensive player leaves his comfort zone or area, moving quickly toward the quarterback. Their mission is to sack the quarterback or the ball carrier before they know what hit them. This is a gamble; if the play does not work, the cornerback or safety will likely be behind the ball (which is a no-no).

Blocking: An offensive player prevents a defensive player from getting to the ball by touching, holding, or bumping any part of the opponent's body. The idea is to stop a defensive player from moving or carrying out his mission, which is to stop the ball carrier. Illegal blocks include clipping, chopping, or hitting below the waist.

Types of blocks:

➣ *Cross block*: Two offensive lineman cross in front of each other, blocking each other's man.

➣ *Cross body block*: An offensive lineman hurls himself horizontally across the chest of a defender.

➣ *Screen*: Offensive lineman gets between a defender and the ball carrier. This gives the ball carrier more time to move downfield.

Bomb: A bomb is any long, arching pass. A successful bomb can make up yards quickly to get to the first down or score a touchdown before time expires. The receiver must be able to concentrate on watching the football and adjust his foot pattern accordingly. Player moves in the direction of where the ball is headed. Remember this is football, not rocket science. The receiver should be able to look at the ball in the air, figure out where it is going to come down, and run underneath it to catch it.

Bootleg: A play used by the quarterback to deceive the defense. The quarterback starts off slow, pretending he has handed the ball off, then instead spins around and runs like a demon down the field. Or he may opt to throw the ball. A bootleg play may also be referred to as the:

➣ hidden ball trick;

➣ razzle-dazzle play;

➣ end around the hocus-pocus play;

➤ double-dealing hoodwink snicker play.

Bread and Butter Play: A team's favorite play normally used to advance the ball.

Break: A receiver manages to get away from the bad guy in an attempt to catch the football. Bottom line: The receiver is all by his little ole self, and if the football is thrown in his vicinity, he better catch it.

Broken play: A broken play is kind of like when you are set for a quiet romantic dinner in front of the fireplace and the in-laws pop in. In other words, play not run according to the original game plan, possibly the result of an offensive player blowing his assignment.

In this situation, if the play is broken the player who blew his assignment may or may not be taken to task for his error or husband is given an ear full when the in-laws pop in, even if it was out of his control.

Bump-and-run: Nothing like bumping and grinding. Bumping and running is a maneuver used by a pass defensive player who hits a receiver within 10 yards of the line of scrimmage in an attempt to slow him down so he can't get to the pass. On the other hand, bumping and grinding is a technique to keep two bodies warm or to stimulate some "other action."

Canadian Football League (CFL): The Canadian's interpretation of American football. The season culminates with the Grey Cup.

Catch: Taking possession of a live ball while in flight (it's alive, it's alive). For a catch to be good it must be caught within the boundaries of the field and not touch the field of play.

Cavemen theory: Men resorting to their prehistoric roots, including making noises or bodily gestures at the television, players, or coaches.

Clipping: An illegal play which, depending on the type of clipping, can draw as much as a 15-yard loss.

➤ Charging into or falling onto the back or across the back of the legs of an opponent who is not running with the ball or pretending to be a runner. Ouch, this could break the poor guy's legs. As you might figure, this is a penalty which draws a 15-yard loss.

➤ Using one's hands or arms to push against an opponent's back. If the clipping is above the waist, a 5-yard loss is assessed.

The official must see the infraction for a clipping penalty to be called. To say it another way, he cannot call what he does not see, so no matter how loud or obnoxious the crowd is, or even if the player's performance is worthy of an Academy Award nomination, if the official does not see it, he cannot call it.

Conference: The methodology of how teams are grouped. In professional football, there are two conferences, the American Football

Conference (AFC) and the National Football Conference (NFC). Within each conference there are three divisions: Central, Eastern, and Western.

Cutback: A runner quickly and abruptly changes his direction against the flow to move into the defensive territory. Do not confuse this with a disoriented runner. The zigzag runner knows exactly what he is doing and where he would like to end up.

Dead ball: A dead ball is a ball that is no longer in play; this usually occurs after the play is over. Conversely a live ball is one that is in play, which happens after the ball is snapped. Oh, so logical.

Declined penalty: Sometimes it is more advantageous for the team who is awarded the penalty yardage to decline the penalty rather than accept it. For example, if the penalty was assessed on fourth down and the offense did not make the necessary yardage, why would any defensive coach in his right mind give the offense another shot at fourth down?

Defensive holding: Holding the offensive player before the ball has reached the opponent. This is done in an attempt to stop a player from catching or getting to the ball. Defensive holding is worth the penalty if it stops the opponent from scoring.

Delay of game: A ball is ready for play after the referee has placed it for a down. A team has seconds to start the play. Should a team not execute within this time period the referee will charge a delay of game penalty. This results in a 5-yard loss. Delay of game is sometimes used as a tactic to psyche the other team out and is worth losing 5 yards.

Disqualified player: A player not eligible to play in a game or who has been kicked off the team. In high school and college, players must maintain a certain grade point average. Additionally high school players must maintain certain citizenship marks. For more specifics, consult the schools athletic director or call the NCAA Hotline.

Dive: A basic speed play whereby the quarterback takes the football from the center. He then pivots and hands the football to the fullback, who runs with a myopic view of the end zone.

Division: In college football it is a grouping of teams: Division I, Division II and Division III. Division I has the most competitive teams whereas Division III has the least competitive. In professional football there are three groupings, the Eastern, Central and Western Division. Of the 16 regular season games, a team plays each team in the division twice; once on their home turf and the other, on their opponent's turf. Also called a home-and-home series. This theoretically promotes rivalries among the teams in the same division.

Double coverage: Two players cover one offensive player.

Down/loss of a down: A down starts with a legal snap and ends with a dead ball. Loss of a down is the loss of the right to repeat a down as a result of the penalty. Some penalties require the teams to replay the down in which the violation occurred.

Down the Field (downfield): The direction the opponent is going when trying to score the big one.

Drama: A basic requirement for all football players, and crucial in certain situations. For example, having a kicker act as though a defensive player ran into him after a kickoff or punt in an attempt to draw a penalty, or getting "clipped" or acting in a "decoy" role to get the other team penalized, is essential in setting the right scene (a winning scene).

Draw: The quarterback pretends to drop back as if he is going to pass downfield. As a result, the linebackers also drop back waiting to see which offensive player is the lucky recipient of the quarterback's throw. Then the sneaky quarterback hands it off to the running back.

Drive: The series of plays a team puts together to score the big touchdown.

Drop back: After the quarterback takes the snap, he takes a few steps backward into an area called the pocket to get ready to throw the ball. Hopefully the offensive line can protect the quarterback until he can get rid of the ball.

Duck: Not a cute little aquatic bird that makes a "quack quack" sound. In football it is a throw that wobbles or spins end over end, rather than in a spiral form.

Eligible receiver: Offensive player legally permitted to catch a forward pass. The quarterback and the lineman are not legally permitted to catch the pass unless they notify the referee ahead of time. Once the referee is notified, these players must also position themselves 1 yard behind the line of scrimmage before the snap.

Encroachment: The defense's version of offsides or could be viewed as the defenses "bubble." Here's why: An offensive player, except for the center, cannot have any part of his body in or over the neutral zone. However, the defense can cross this zone as many times as they want as long as they can get back on their side without touching an offensive player and before the ball is snapped. The defense quite often will move in an attempt to distract the offense.

End: The offensive or defensive player positioned (standing) at the end of the line.

End zone: The end zones are 10 yards deep and are located at each end of the field. The goal posts are located in the center of the end zone. This is traditionally where the touchdown dance is performed.

Extra Point(s): The extra point(s) scored after a touchdown; can be either a 2-point conversion or the point-after touchdown.

Facemask: When a player grabs the head mask (bars around front of helmet) in an attempt to tackle the ball carrier. This can be a very dangerous play. When the facemasking is flagrant, a team is penalized 15 yards. If the facemasking is unintentional (an accident), the team is penalized 5 yards.

When a player grabs an opponent's facemask, watch the player's head as it is whipped to one side while his body is whipped to the opposite side.

Fair catch: When the kick-returner decides on just catching the football after a punt or a kickoff rather than trying to run the ball up field. To signal a fair catch the kick-returner waves one arm in the air before he catches the football. Once the fair catch is signaled, an opponent cannot hit or touch him.

False start: The offense must be in a ready or set position (hands on or near the ground) before the snap of the ball for a full second. During this time, the interior lineman may not move his hands or make any other sudden movements.

The purpose of this rule is so the defense is not tricked into crossing the line of scrimmage early. Defensive players know that once the offense goes into motion, the play has started. Thus the offenses movement becomes the signal to attack. The center may move the ball to get a handle on it, but he cannot pick it up, stand up, or abruptly move his shoulders or head. The running back must also be set for a full second. Only one offensive player may be "in motion" moving sideways or backwards.

Field Goal: Worth 3 points when at the appropriate time the kicker can boot the oval-looking ball through the two uprights.

First Down: The first of only four chances to move the football 10 yards or score a touchdown. If a team moves the ball 10 yards but does not score a touchdown the team has earned another first down.

Forward Motion: Movement toward opposing team's goal line.

Forward progress: When the player running with the ball gets stopped, but the defense cannot bring the tenacious ball carrier down. Rather than going down, the player keeps getting pushed back. The official will usually blow his whistle and spot the ball where the forward progress is stopped, not the spot where the player hits the turf (ground).

Free agent: Players not signed to a contract. In this situation the multi-million wannabe can sign with any team that makes him a worthy offer.

Fumble: Player loses control of the ball. When the ball is dropped on the ground, either team can recover it. If the defense recovers, it is commonly called a "turnover." After a fumble, the official determines which team has possession of the ball. If at the bottom of the pile, the official finds both a defensive and offensive player with their mitts on the ball, then the tie goes to the offense.

Coaches hate fumbles. The ball carrier should practice what to do when this happens. Fumbles happen to the best. Practicing can actually minimize the goof. For example, the receiver should know how to cover up the loose ball, and he should know how to position himself so not to let a defender get his hands on it.

Goal line: Is the vertical plane that separates the field of play from the end zone.

Hail Mary: When time expires, the quarterback throws the ball as high as he can into a crowd of offensive players in the end zone, hoping and praying one of his receivers comes down with it. If the quarterback has said enough Hail Mary's, his guy catches the ball.

Halfback option: Similar to an option except the halfback sweeps around. The halfback can pass or continue to run with the ball.

Hand off: A running play where the quarterback hands the football off to a back. Remember a back is an offensive player or more formally called a halfback or fullback.

Hang-time: The time a punt is in the air. The longer the better, that way the punt team can get to the punt-returner before he can advance the football.

Hash marks: Two broken lines, twenty-four inches in length, which divide the field into thirds. When the ball goes out of bounds or is downed near a sideline, the official places the ball on the nearest hash mark.

Heisman Trophy: Trophy awarded to the best college football player in the country. Depending on the notoriety of the athlete, the trophy could eventually be worth a small mint.

Hike: The act of handing or passing the football from the center to the quarterback to start each play from the line of scrimmage.

Holding: Holding, clamping, grasping, or restraining the opponent so he cannot move. This is considered an unfair advantage, not an act of endearment. If seen by a referee, this results in the yellow flag being thrown.

Defensive holding is called when he defensive player throws a bear hug around an offensive player to stop him from going where he wants to go.

Home game: A game played in a team's own stadium. A home-team advantage can give a team favorable advantage since you have the crowds pumping up the home team and yelling at inconvenient times to distract the visiting team.

Huddle: The huddle is a 100-year-old tradition. Players use this special time together to discuss and conceal the next play from their opponents. Players will bend over slightly, forming a circle or oval shape while they call out the next play. This stance keeps the enemy from reading the offensive players lips. They are very careful to conceal the signs from their enemy. In the offensive huddle, the quarterback calls the play. Within the defensive huddle, the team calls the defensive plays and hypes each other up for the next play. A huddle is similar to when men at half-time converge around the buffet table to discuss the highlights of the game.

Hurdling: Leapfrogging over an opponent. It's not allowed.

Illegal block: A player cannot block the opponent below the waist. Similar to boxing, where you cannot hit your opponent below the belt or in the nuts. There is one exception to this rule. If the opponent is in the "free zone," which is 4 yards laterally, and 3 yards deep from the ball, the defensive player can block the opponent below the waist. But he still cannot hit him in the nuts.

Illegal forward pass: The quarterback is not allowed to throw the ball forward once he has crossed the line of scrimmage. Should the quarterback cross the line of scrimmage, he can only throw a lateral (sideways) or backward pass.

There are five types of passes considered illegal:

➤ A forward pass thrown after the possession has changed to the other team (as on a kickoff or punt return).

➤ A pass thrown by the quarterback after he has crossed the line of scrimmage.

➤ A pass caught or batted by an ineligible receiver beyond the neutral zone.

➤ A pass thrown with the purpose of getting rid of the ball before the quarterback gets sacked. This is called "intentional grounding."

➤ A pass thrown into an area not occupied by an eligible offensive receiver.

Illegal motion: This penalty is called when an offensive player is not set (motionless, stiff as a board) for the full second before the snap. The most common type of illegal motion is when two offensive players are in motion. Remember, only one offensive player can be in motion.

Incomplete pass: A pass that is not caught. The ball hits the ground before it is caught. An incomplete pass may be due to a lousy pass, lousy hands, or the disruption of concentration experienced by a receiver or quarterback who hears the "pitter-patter" of a 300-pound tackle's feet.

Ineligible receiver: A receiver that should not be downfield. This occurs when an overzealous interior lineman breaks downfield before the ball is thrown.

Infraction: A rule that has been broken.

Instant reply: Used only in professional football. A coach can "challenge" the officials ruling as long as it is not a judgment call. If the call is upheld, meaning no change, the coach is charged a time-out. If the official changes the ruling, the coach is not charged the time-out.

Interception: When a defender catches the pass instead of the offense. When this happens, the offense quickly must think of themselves as the defense.

Interference: When a defensive or offensive player interferes with a player trying to catch the pass. The defensive player cannot bump or grab the offensive player before the ball reaches him. Both players must have a chance to make the play.

Key: A clue used to determine the offensive play to be run. This may include watching one or two offensive players whose movement usually will indicate the type of play to be run.

Kick: Intentionally kicking the ball. Types of kicks:

➢ *Free kick*: used to put the ball in play at the start of each half, after a successful field goal and after a point after touchdown attempt.

➢ *Place kick*: the ball is kicked from a fixed position on the ground, such as a tee. The place kick can be used for a scrimmage kick, a kickoff, or a free kick following a safety.

➢ *Punt*: the kicker drops the ball and kicks it before it hits the ground. A punt is used in fourth down situations in an attempt to gain better field position.

Kicking Tee: A plastic contour mold used to hold the ball prior to the kickoff.

Lateral: A ball carrier shovels the ball sideways or backward, usually thrown underhand, in an attempt to avoid being tackled.

Line of scrimmage: The imaginary line that runs from the spot where the ball is placed to start a play to each sideline.

Lineman: A player, offensive or defensive, who lines up within 1 yard of the line of scrimmage.

Live ball: A ball in play, indicating that the ball has been legally snapped or free kicked and that a down is in progress. A live ball indicates that the play has officially started.

Loose ball: A thrown or kicked ball that has not yet touched the ground, or a ball which is bouncing around on the field and neither team can seem to get their paws on it.

Man-in-motion: This is not a man trying to pick up a date. Before the snap, one offensive player can move prior to the snap. His movement is legal as long as he moves in a lateral or backward direction from the line of scrimmage.

Man-to-man: Not what you think. Defensive player is assigned to a specific offensive player to cover. Used instead of a "zone" defense.

Mascot: A person, animal, or object that represents the team in hopes of bringing them good luck.

Monday Night Football: Similar to an A.A. meeting. Sacrificial places where football junkies can meet, discuss football stuff, and watch one last game of football for the week. That is, of course, if we are not lucky enough to have a Thursday night game.

Muff: When the kicker or punter tries to kick the ball but misses. The ball rolls 1 to 2 yards. Not a pretty sight.

National Collegiate Athletic Association (NCAA): The college rules committee that establishes the guidelines that players must follow to be eligible for collegiate sports.

National Football League (NFL): The oldest football organization in the United States which was established in 1922. The league is divided into two major competitive groups: the American Football Conference (AFL) and the National Football Conference (NFL). The season climaxes with the big one; no not that one, the Super Bowl.

Neutral zone: The imaginary line, the width of a football, that runs along the line of scrimmage. The neutral zone separates the offense and the defense before the play begins. Once the ball has been snapped, both teams can begin to attack.

Nickel back: Has nothing to do with money or getting a refund for watching a crummy game. This is a defensive formation. A fifth defensive back lines up on the line, replacing a defensive lineman. The nickel back can either drop into pass coverage or he can rush the passer. This formation puts more pressure on the quarterback and offers a more aggressive attack.

Offside: When any part of a player's body crosses the line of scrimmage before the ball is snapped. This infraction draws a 5-yard penalty.

Open receiver: A receiver not covered by a defensive player. In other words, he's open, willing, and able to catch the football.

Option: An offensive player runs around behind the line of scrimmage looking and praying for an open receiver to throw the ball to. The option play is an attempt to keep the defense off balance because they do not know what the offense is going to do until the last minute. There are two types of options:

> ➤ The quarterback takes the snap, rolls out (running parallel to the line), and runs like hell to gain the yards or score the touchdown (quarterback option).

> ➤ The halfback takes the hand-off or pitch from the quarterback, rolls out (running parallel to the line), and attempts to gain the yards or the touchdown (halfback option), similar to the quarterback option except the halfback is attempting to move the ball.

Out-of-bounds: The area outside the sidelines or end lines. Once a player goes out-of-bounds, even if it was an accident, the play is over.

Pass: The football sails through the air to its intended target: wide receiver, flanker, tight end, or one of its running backs. The initial direction of the pass determines whether it is a forward or a backward pass.

Pass defender: A defensive player covering the receiver who thinks he is going to catch the football.

Pass patterns or pass routes: Pre-determine play designed by an offensive coordinator or coach. With the pre-determine play, players know exactly what they are supposed to do, how they are supposed to do it, and what is expected of them.

Passing play: The quarterback takes the snap and steps backward into his imaginary area, called the pocket. He then throws the ball forward to an eligible receiver. The receiver attempts to catch and advance the ball.

Pass protection: Offensive players attempting to protect and give the quarterback more time to throw the football before the defensive players can get in his face or tackle him.

Pass rush: An attempt to sack the quarterback.

Penalty: The punishment given when a player breaks one of the sacred rules.

Personal foul: An infraction that exhibits unnecessary roughness that could result in injury to a player. The penalty for a personal foul is a loss of 15 yards.

Picked off: Plain and simple, an interception; a very bad, bad thing.

Pitch out: A play in which the halfback moves to the outside very quickly. The ball is then pitched to him as he darts toward the outside (sideline).

Play book: Similar to a cookbook. Contains all the vital ingredients to a successful game plan, including plays, positions, and formations.

Play clock: A clock displayed above each team's end zone that limits how much time a team can rest between plays. In professional play the play clock starts at forty seconds. The next play must start before the clock counts down to zero. In college a play must resume within twenty-five seconds after the preceding play has ended. After an injury, change of possession, or time-out a play must resume within twenty-five seconds.

Pocket: In a pass play, it is the imaginary area formed by the offensive linemen in front and around the quarterback so he can successfully pass the ball.

Point after touchdown: Worth 1 point if the kicker can boot the ball between the two uprights. The point after touchdown is attempted after a touchdown.

Possession: The team with the ball.

Post: A pass deep across the middle toward the goal post.

Punt: The kicker drops the ball and kicks it before it hits the ground. Usually done on fourth down situations.

Pylon: The short orange post at each of the end zone's four corners. Usually made from some sort of plastic material so when a player dives, rolls, or crashes into it, it does not injure the player.

Quarterback scramble: Not an egg dish. The quarterback is chased out of the pocket. A resourceful receiver knows how to adjust and get open so the scrambling quarterback can successfully pass the ball to him before he gets sacked.

Recipe: The formula for preparing and winning at football:

Football Success
Serves an unlimited number of spectators
Stadium
Equipment
Coaches
Players
Strategy

Rile up spectators. At stadium, make sure all the equipment is in place, players have been carefully selected, players are properly prepared, and coaches have analyzed and prepared an appropriate strategy for the opponent. Mix and blend running plays according to situation. Stir in passing plays to keep the opponent confused. Continue to pour on team's strengths. Add second and third string players when first string players are exhausted or hurt. Cook and keep pressure on until time has expired. After a win, the spectators should celebrate gratuitously. Work time: sixty minutes (professional) or forty-eight minutes (high school). Total time: 180 minutes (professional) or 120 minutes (high school).

Recovery: A player gains possession of the football after it has been fumbled. The player who recovers the ball after a fumble gets lots of kudos from his teammates including pats on the rear and head butts. Coaches and fans love when their team recovers the ball and really hate when their stupid team loses the ball.

Return: An attempt by a player to move the football.

Reverse: The running back runs to one side and the defense runs after him. The running back then hands off the ball to another player going the other way. Watch out for these tricky plays.

Rollout: The quarterback moves outside of the pocket in an attempt to get the football to a receiver.

Rookie: First-year player, usually green around the gills.

Roughing the kicker: Illegal contact with the kicker or the punter. With the kicker's foot extended you can imagine how vulnerable this poor guy is should an opponent come in contact with him.

Roughing the passer: Illegal contact with the quarterback during or after a pass. Since the quarterback is concentrating on completing the pass and not on protecting himself, the quarterback is in a vulnerable position and could get seriously hurt.

Running play: The quarterback hands or tosses the ball backward to either the running back or the fullback. The player with the ball attempts to run as fast as his legs will carry him while at the same time dodging the oncoming opponent. If he is successful, the running play can result in a touchdown.

Sack: The quarterback is put on his rump behind the line of scrimmage before he can pass the ball. This is a defense's dream and an offense's nightmare.

Safety: When an offensive player is tackled or ruled down in their own end zone. Looks similar to a touchdown but is in the wrong end zone and is worthy of only 2 points.

Scoreboard: The board at either end of the field, which displays the score during and after the game. The scoreboard displays the current quarter, the down, and the minutes remaining. When the score is displayed on television the team on the bottom is always the home team. A television scoreboard will also display the word "flag" when a penalty is called. Pay attention because sometimes you can yell "flag" before the guys can read or see what happen.

Screen pass: The defensive line rushes the quarterback. The quarterback then lobs the ball over their heads to an eligible receiver, usually a running back.

Secondary: No, not the second string. These are the defensive players lined up in the backfield. In football lingo, these are the cornerbacks, safeties, or deep backs.

Shift: After the huddle and before taking position, one or more offensive player moves to assume a new position. The players on the offensive line cannot move until the quarterback has received the ball.

Shoestring tackle: In an attempt to bring down the ball carrier, a player grabs the ball carrier's shoelaces.

Shotgun: Offensive formation. The quarterback lines up 4 to 5 yards behind the center to receive the snap. This lineup means the play will probably be a pass play. The shotgun formation normally allows the quarterback additional time to get the pass off.

Sideline: The boundary line that runs the length of the field along each side. When a player touches or crosses the sideline the play is over.

Slant: The defensive linemen position themselves head on to the offensive linemen. Initially this formation is used to intimidate the offense. However, when the ball is snapped, the defensive players rush around the offensive line in an attempt to get to the ball carrier.

Snap: The center "hikes" or moves the football to the quarterback.

Spearing: Intentionally using the helmet as a weapon in an attempt to push an opponent away. Spearing an opponent can cause severe injury. This is really poor sportsmanship and is illegal.

Spike: A player throws the ball to the ground. A quarterback sometimes spikes the ball when his team is out of time-outs and he wants to stop the clock. Other times a spiked ball will be thrown to celebrate a touchdown.

Spiral: A football thrown or kicked that has a continuous spin while in flight. The spin usually helps propel the football.

Spot: The place where the official has marked the ball dead. Also could be the name of a player's or coach's best friend. Otherwise known as his dog.

Starter: Player who starts the game. The first player to play a position during the game.

Straight arm (or stiff arm): A move used by the running backs where they extend one arm with palm outward to avoid being tackled. If a player is not careful he could potentially break his arm. (Seems like a dumb way to stop a 250-pound mad man bearing down on you.)

Stripped: Ball is forcibly removed from a player's possession. All of his clothes stay on.

Substitute: Player who comes in for a starter. Also known as a second or third stringer, or even a bench warmer.

Sweep: Nothing to do with brooms or house cleaning. Running play that goes wide laterally (width of football field) and tries to run around the defense.

Tackle: Act of trying to bring a player with or without the ball to the ground.

Telestrator: The tool that allows television commentators the ability to chart, illustrate, and exaggerate what just happened in the last play. John Madden's (the infamous television commentator and football legend) true talents are exhibited when he uses the telestrator.

Three and Out: The offensive team is unsuccessful in moving the ball 10 yards and is forced to punt on fourth down. Considered lousy football for the offense and excellent football for the defense.

Third and Long: Third down situation. On third down, the offense is more than 5 yards from making a first down.

Time-out: There are potentially twelve time-outs, six for each team. A team cannot be greedy and use all six time-outs in one half. Instead they are allowed only three time-outs per half. The coach designates a defensive player who is responsible for calling the time-out. On offense the player responsible for calling time-outs is the quarterback.

Touchback: Points are not associated with a touchback. It is always fun to listen to the armchair quarterback yell in complete disgust when a touchback occurs. Why? Because after a touchback the football is brought out from the end zone and placed on the 20-yard line, effectively giving the opponent an extra 19 yards.

Examples of a touchback are:

➤ When the ball is kicked in or through the end zone. In the pros, if the ball is kicked into the end zone, the receiver can either run the ball out or kneel down and take the touchback.

➤ In high school ball, a free or scrimmage kick that touches anything behind the goal line results in a touchback.

➤ If the defensive team intercepts the ball in the end zone and the guy who catches the pass chooses to hang around and just enjoy the moment rather than run the ball out.

Touchdown: When a team crosses the opponent's goal line—oh yeah, don't forget the opponent has to have the football. It does not matter if the ball is caught, run, or recovered in the end zone it still ends up being worth 6 points.

Touchdown dance: Dance routine performed after a touchdown. Usually choreographed ahead of time. No music is necessary. The touchdown dance generally involves some very unorthodox moves. In high school or college, doing a touchdown dance is considered unsportsmanlike conduct and earns a 15-yard penalty. So you lads should wait till the Christmas formal to perform your dance steps.

Trash talking: Saying a lot of bad words or insulting the opposing player. The point is to make the opponent feel inferior. A rudimentary form of intimidation, however football players think this is a sophisticated form.

Tripping: Player extends his foot or leg outward with the intent to cause the other player to land on his butt or plant his head face first into the grass. Not a very nice or polite thing to do, even in the game of football.

Turnover: The involuntary loss of the football. A very bad, bad thing.

2-point conversion: After a touchdown a coach may opt to put more than 1 measly point on the board. A 2-point conversion looks and smells just like a touchdown attempt.

World League of American Football (WLAF): London's interpretation of American football. The season climaxes with the World Bowl.

Yardage: The distance gained or lost on a play. It is measured from the line of scrimmage. Also the material used to make the uniforms.

Yellow Line: The line shown on television that shows where the offensive team must reach to earn the next series of downs. A very helpful visual tool even for the football buff.

CHAPTER 2

GAME OVERVIEW

As Al Davis, owner of the Oakland Raiders (whose home was in Oakland, then Los Angeles, and then back to Oakland—and they say women can't make up their minds)—would say, "Just win, baby!" Now here's the really tough part to that (not):

> ➤ A team wins by putting more points on the board than the other team;

> ➤ Touchdowns are good;

> ➤ Fumbles are bad (real bad);

> ➤ Our male counterparts are going to make complete jerks of themselves coaching the game, refereeing, or yelling at the players. Keep in mind this is all done from the comfort of the couch or the safety of the bleachers.

When players are said to have heart, it means they want to win at all costs. Players without heart should not be on the field. If players are not on the field to kill and/or maim, then they should not be playing the game. Football is a brutal and vicious sport.

To play the game it takes two teams, the good team and the bad team. Within each team there are three types of players:

> ➤ Offensive players, who have the football;

> ➤ Defensive players, who are trying to get the football;

➤ Special teams, who either have the football or are trying to get the football, depending on whether they are on offense or defense.

Not all three teams can be on the field at the same time. The players (like good little boys) must take their turn at getting to play. The situation, play, or strategy dictates which players get to take the field.

Dinnertime has many of the same characteristics as the game of football. When dinner is ready, the family will sit at either the dinner table or in front of the boob tube. Whichever the case, the family (players) waits with bated breath for the fine cuisine to be served (start of the game). Mom (offensive player/quarterback) serves (starts) the food and starts the game. Her strategy is to serve everyone (score) as quickly as possible without dropping the food (fumbling), serving the food cold (incomplete pass), or without serving one of the family members out of turn (illegal procedure). Mom (offensive player/quarterback) tries to pass her infamous lumpy white potatoes (football) to the youngest son, Fran (offensive player/receiver). Otis, the middle son (defensive player/linebacker), pays close attention to the direction the lumpy potato dish is moving. Otis decides he is not going to wait until Fran (offensive player/receiver) serves himself and attempts to grab (intercept) the lumpy potatoes. In an attempt to maintain order, Dad (offensive player/guard) grabs (blocks) Otis' hand. Dad's action causes both sons to lose their grip of the potato dish (football) causing the dish to drop to the floor (fumble). All of this takes place in two to three seconds (at least in my family).

In summary:

➤ Mom was unsuccessful in passing the potato dish (incomplete pass);

➤ The youngest son, Fran, did not get any potatoes (no yards gained);

➤ The middle son, Otis, did his job by stopping the movement of the lumpy potato dish (successful defensive play);

➤ Dad (offensive player/guard) was successful in his attempt to stop Otis´ (defensive player/linebacker) from intercepting the lumpy potatoes (football);

➤ In fact, Dad caused Fran to drop the potato dish (football) on the floor (fumble);

➤ When all the food is gone, the person who ate the most (gained the most yards and scored the most points) wins.

SAME OLD, SAME OLD

The game of football consists of nothing more than the same old steps over and over again, until one team has more points than the other team. Depending on a number of factors such as time remaining, points on the board, or possession of the ball, the steps may change from a walking pace to a sprint to an all-out mad dash. However the basic steps of moving one foot in front of the other remains the same.

The similarities between making dinner and the game of football are scary. The first step in making dinner is to figure out what to make. In football the coach has to figure out what play to run. This is tough since you know one of the picky eaters won't even touch it (failure to move the football), the food will be inhaled in less than two minutes (touchdown), Dad will end up eating everyone's leftovers (interception), or there isn't enough time to fix dinner (two-minute warning). Frankly it doesn't make any difference if you use a new recipe or create one from scratch (choose a running play versus a pass play) or, for that matter, use leftovers from earlier in the week or get take-out (punt the ball on fourth down or attempt to make a first down). You can be as creative as you want in getting dinner on the table. However the only thing that counts is getting dinner on the table before everyone loses their sense of humor. Although it may not be a masterpiece, at least everyone will be full. In football jargon this is called "winning ugly."

Following are the basic steps in a football game:

TO START THE GAME: The special team who elected "to receive":	The special team who elected to kick the ball:
Catches and runs with ball.	Kicks the ball to the other team.
IF THE OFFENSIVE TEAM:	**THEN THE DEFENSIVE TEAM:**
Catches the ball.	Tackles the big boy with the ball.
Four tries (downs) to move the ball 10 yards.	Annihilates the big boy with the ball.
If successful at moving the ball 10 yards, they will get another four tries to move the ball or get inside the end zone.	Kills anyone close to the ball. (Are you seeing a trend yet?)
If not successful at moving the ball 10 yards, then the coach has three choices: Punt the ball. Attempt field goal. Attempt for needed yards. If the offense is unsuccessful, then the offense runs off field.	Block the punt. Block the field goal. Kill anyone close to the ball. Scratch that—just kill anyone. Defense runs off the field.
IN SUMMARY: The offense runs around avoiding the defense until they get into the end zone or run out of downs (or run out of time).	The defense kills anyone close to the ball.

The above repeats itself until time expires. When time expires, the team with the most points on the board wins. Nothing to it, even a Neanderthal can understand it. That's probably why men have no problem grasping the concepts.

CHAPTER 3

WARM IT UP

Preseason games (not to be confused with pre-game activities) precede a game and have nothing to do with the game of football. Pre-game activities include:

➤ Preparing for an inside game;

➤ Preparing for an outside game;

➤ Introducing the teams;

➤ Singing the national anthem;

➤ The coin toss.

Preseason games, on the other hand, are nothing more than practice games. They are practice games for the coaches, players, and fans.

Preseason games serve three main functions:

➤ They give coaches an opportunity to evaluate the team's strengths and weaknesses. After a preseason game, the coach makes the necessary adjustments, keeping the players who cut the mustard or cutting those players who are full of bologna. Players making the cut make up the first, second, or special teams. In professional ball it also determines which players make the roster and which players are sent home for a very long and lonely season;

➤ They help players work together as a team;

➤ They help female fans who have a hard time getting into football cope with the thought of another lonely and dreary football season. (That is until they have read this book.)

Keep in mind a team can lose its preseason games and still win the league or a conference title. In high school football, the teams' overall standings (including preseason games) dictates where, when, and who you play in the playoffs. In college the team with the best record plays in a bowl game. Playing in a bowl game is comparable to a professional team playing in the Super Bowl. It means big bucks to colleges, and for players it brings national and professional recognition. In professional ball, the winners of the American Football Conference (AFC) and the National Football Conference (NFC) play in the grand enchilada of them all, the Super Bowl.

Coaching a team to play in either the Super Bowl or in a bowl game is extremely important to the owners and colleges. Owners demand performance; if a team isn't winning, stadium attendance drops drastically. If a team can't fill the stadium, owners and colleges are not making money. Don't let anyone tell you otherwise, football is big business. A coach is usually allowed a couple of losing seasons before he finds himself pounding the pavement for another job, which might be another coaching position, being a television commentator, doing commercial endorsements, or retiring. It is a "dog eat dog" business with absolutely no room for failure. In football coaches are held accountable for the team's performance.

Should a coach land another coaching job you may find yourself asking why would one team want another team's discard. Owners justify such selections by saying the new coach "Offers a better fit with the teams psyche," or "Shares the same philosophies as management." But what the owners don't say is the new coach doesn't mind being a puppet as long as he is given a chance to coach.

Bottom line: Owners have too much say in the daily operations of their football teams. Since owners are not coaches, owners tend to make lousy coaching decisions.

TEAM STANDINGS

Tracking a team's performance is simple. Leave it to the male mystique to make it seem more complex than it really is but this is as tough as it gets. After every game played the results of the game are recorded in one of three columns. The first column is marked when a team wins, the second marked for a loss, and the third marked for ties. That's it!

This overly complicated method of record keeping is commonly referred to as "standings." With this methodology anyone interested can read and compare one team's results with another. Standings are similar to a report card in that it reflects a student's performance for a particular grading period. However, by the time you receive a report card, it usually is too late to improve the grade unless you can persuade or negotiate a deal with the instructor. Standings, on the other hand, are current, and when changes are made, they could have dramatic results on the overall standings.

Savvy coaches make strategic changes to improve the team's performance. These strategic changes might include replacing deadweight players with more productive players, or rearranging players to new and more exciting positions.

Following are a couple of basic examples of how to read the standings and interpret the hidden meaning:

TEAM	WIN	LOSE	TIE
Monkeys	1	10	0
Donkeys	8	1	1

The Monkeys are a team in serious trouble. In fact they stink. They have lost ten games and won only one. If the coach does not take drastic steps to improve his team's performance, he may be out beating the bushes for a new job next season.

The Donkeys, on the other hand, are in very good shape. They have won eight, lost one, and tied one.

With this gigantic bit of knowledge, you can read any team's standings. Additionally you can calculate the feasibility of a team improving its standings. Most importantly you can avoid asking dumb questions, such as:

➢ "What place are we in?"

➢ "How many games are we out of first?"

➢ "What do all those numbers mean?"

➢ "Who cares about all those stupid numbers anyway?"

TEAM STATISTICS

It would seem once you knew the team's standings you have all the information you need. No way. It is not good enough to just win the game. The coaches need to be able to scrutinize a player's performance. Management needs to be able to analyze and dissect both the coaches and the team's performance. And the football junkie needs every morsel to further critique the players and coaches to successfully participate in the football pool. Thus someone has ingeniously assembled numbers, averages, and percentages to keep everyone happy. Following are some of the statistics available:

Passing statistics:
➤ How many yards did the quarterback attempt to throw the ball? (Att)
➤ Of those yards how many were completed? (Comp)
➤ What was the percentage of those completed? (Pct)
➤ How many yards were gained on the pass thrown? (Yds)
➤ How many resulted in a touchdown? (TD)
➤ How many were intercepted? (Int)
➤ What was the longest pass completed? (Long)
➤ What was the overall success of the quarterback? (Rating)

Rushing statistics:
➤ How many attempts did a player run with the ball? (Att)
➤ How many yards did a player carry the ball? (Yds)
➤ What was the average number of yards gained? (Avg)
➤ What was the longest gain on the rushing attempt? (Long)
➤ How many times did the player cross the goal line? (TD)

Receiving statistics:
➤ How many times did the player catch the ball? (No.)
➤ How many yards were gained on the play? (Yds)
➤ What was the average number of yards gained when a player caught the ball? (Avg)
➤ What was the longest gain on the play? (Long)
➤ How many of them resulted in a touchdown? (TD)

Statistics for the offensive players:
➤ How many field goals were attempted? (FGA)
➤ How many field goals did the kicker make? (FG)
➤ How many extra points were attempted and how many were made? (XPA)/(XP)
➤ How points did a player score? (Pts)
➤ What was the average number of yards of a punter's punts? (Gross Avg)
➤ What was the average number of yards gained by a kickoff or punt-returner from where he gains possession?

Statistics for the defensive players:

➤ How many passes were intercepted? (Interceptions)
➤ How many sacks were made? (Sacks). Should two players combine for a sack, each player gets half of a credit.

Team statistics:

➤ How many games has a team won, loss, or tied? (Win-Loss-Tied Record)
➤ How many times did a team gain 10 yards in four or less plays? (First Downs)
➤ How many times did the team earn the next set of downs? (3rd Down Efficiency)
➤ How many turnovers were made? (Turnovers)
➤ How many penalties were assessed against a team, and what was the total number of yards it was penalized? (Penalties/Yards)
➤ What was the cumulative time, measured by the game clock, that a team was on offense? (Time of Possession).

Thank goodness we have technology to compile, sort, and store this vital information.

CHAPTER 4

DA POINTS

As discussed earlier, the team with the most points on the board is the winner. The offensive team tries to put points on the board by running or throwing the football to a receiver in the "end zone." This should not be confused with a home run (baseball), hoop (basketball), hole-in-one (golf), or go-o-o-al (soccer). The defensive team tries to prevent the barrage of meat coming across the line of scrimmage and moving the football downfield.

There are several ways to put points on the scoreboard:

Touchdown	6 points
Field goal	3 points
Safety	2 points
2-point conversion	2 points
Point after or extra point	1 point

THE TOUCHDOWN

As you can see, the fastest way to put points on the board is with a touchdown. The touchdown is earned when a player moves any part of the football into the end zone. Moving the ball into the end zone includes carrying, passing, running, or diving with the ball. For the official to call a touchdown, only the football must cross into the end zone.

Think of it as an imaginary glass wall that is only broken by a rubber football—not by flesh, bones, pads, helmets, or the like. The football is what counts, not the player. Suppose a player slides feet first into the end zone with the ball tucked underneath his left arm. The player's left arm never crosses the imaginary glass wall. Is this a touchdown? Sorry, but no. The dumb athlete forgot to get the football into the end zone.

A player can actually go completely horizontal, extending only the football through the imaginary glass wall, and the touchdown will count. Close your eyes and imagine a 250-pound ballerina wearing a tutu that weighs about 10 pounds. As part of the dance he extends his body completely vertical to catch the ball thrown into the end zone. Or imagine a gymnast wearing a 10-pound leotard, tucking and rolling over 2100 pounds of flesh and muscle. And you thought these guys were just big.

In addition to the football crossing the end zone, depending on the level of football you are watching there are additional rules for the touchdown to count. For example, in professional ball a player catching a pass in the end zone must have both feet inbounds and have control of the ball before the official can call the touchdown. In high school and college ball, the player needs only one foot inbounds for a legal catch.

In addition to keeping the foot (or feet) inbounds, a player must also control the football for the official to call the touchdown. Controlling the football means the player must catch the football with at least one hand and maintain possession of the ball for a couple of seconds. The player may not juggle or fumble around with the ball. Bottom line: The player must have a secure grasp of the ball for it to be called a legal catch.

The game of football is played within the four corners of the field. A player and the play must be kept on the field at all times. The "feet in bound" rule is an extension of this logic, "keep it on the field." It is not played on the sidelines, in the stadium, or in the locker room. For this reason you will never see a player running down the sidelines, through the locker room, into the stadium, or down the goal post to score the touchdown. The play has to start, stay, and end on the field. A player's piggy toes cannot even be a little teensy-weensy bit out of bounds. Close does not count; the entire foot or feet must be inside the end zone.

Not only can the offense score but the defense can also put points on the board by scoring the big touchdown. This is accomplished when a defensive player makes an interception or recovers a fumble and then runs the ball into his end zone. Once this happens, the defense's offensive team runs onto the field and attempts either the point after (extra point) or a 2-point conversion. Watch the type of players the coach brings on the field. If the coach opts for the extra point he will send in the kicking team. Or if the coach sends in his offensive team, the team will be attempting the 2-point conversion.

26

FIELD GOAL

The field goal is kicked when a team does not have a chance of scoring a touchdown or earning the next set of downs. A successful field goal attempt puts 3 points on the board. Granted it is not 6 points, but anything is better than a big fat zero.

For the field goal to count, the ball must be kicked between and over the cross bar, not around the two uprights, not below, but over the cross bar. The ball can hit an upright and still bounce between the two uprights for the official to call a field goal. After a successful kick, two officials run and stand near the uprights; both officials extend both arms straight over their heads at exactly the same time. This is also the same signal used for a successful touchdown.

To attempt or not to attempt the field goal is an enigma of the football world. Should we go for the touchdown, or should we opt for a paltry field goal? Since points on the board is what determine the winner, a coach normally decides on the surest way to get points on the board. Typically you hear a lot of second-guessing: "Man, the coach should go for the touchdown," "Jeez, he should have gone for the field goal," or "What is he doing, I can't believe he's not going for the 3 points, what an idiot!"

Either way, attempting either the touchdown or the field goal, is a calculated risk. The coach's decision is based on a number of factors, such as the team's field position, the offense's ability to get the ball in the end zone, or the kicker's chances of making the field goal. If the coach does not feel warm and fuzzy because perhaps the team is not close enough to make the field goal, or because he has a lousy kicker, or it is too far to go for the first down, the coach will likely signal for the punting team.

If the field goal is attempted but missed, the opponent's offense takes over at the original line of scrimmage.

If the field goal is blocked, the ball is a live ball until recovered by one of the teams. This is an exciting play. Watch each player scramble to pick up the bouncing and sometimes skipping ball. Should the defense get lucky and pick up the ball, they can technically run the ball downfield for the touchdown. If the offense recovers the ball, they can attempt a first down or run it in for a touchdown.

If you want to participate in meaningful conversations with the big boys, such as "Man, a 48-yard field goal attempt, no way," you need to be able to figure out how long the field goal attempt is. Otherwise you won't be able to make such a commanding statement. Don't worry you don't need a calculator. Just add 14 yards to the spot where the ball is marked dead. For example, if the ball is spotted dead on the 37-yard line, then it is a 51-yard field goal attempt. The reason is because the goal posts are 10 yards past the beginning of the end zone plus 4 yards from where the ball is snapped. It's not rocket science; remember who made up the rules.

SAFETY

The defensive team can also put points on the board by scoring a safety, which is worth a whopping 2 points. The safety most easily recognized is when a defensive player tackles the player with the football in his own end zone.

A safety can occur in a number of ways. The more difficult safeties to recognize occur as follows:

➤ The center hikes the ball over the quarterback's head and the ball goes through the end zone. At dinner Mom (quarterback) asks Fran (center) for a roll (football). Instead of handing the roll to his mother like a gentleman, Frank tosses the roll over his mom's head, off the table (end zone),and onto the floor (through the end zone—a safety). Or if Barney, the dog, jumped up grabbed the roll and ate it, that would be an interception.

➤ On a point after attempt, the kick is blocked. In college ball, either team can pick up the ball and run it into their end zone for a safety. If this should happen in professional or high school ball, the play is over. You (kicker) have the dreaded chore of trying to feed the baby his peas (football). The baby (linebacker) grabs (blocks) the spoon before you can get the peas in his mouth (end zone). The baby then takes the spoon and attempts to feed himself. Although the baby does not get all of the peas in his mouth he is able to get some of them in the mouth (safety). Remember in football you only have to get the football in the end zone, not the entire body.

➤ Like anything else, there are always exceptions. The quarterback gets sacked in the end zone and the ball comes loose. Should the defense recover the fumble, they've scored a touchdown, not a safety! Mom (quarterback) is getting ready to serve dessert (football) in the living room (end zone). Her hands are still wet from doing the dishes. The dessert slips from her hands and onto the living room floor (end zone). Barney, the loveable Lab (defensive player), is quicker than Fran (offensive player) and devours the dessert before anyone can get him to release it (touchdown).

Here are two more examples of a safety that your all-knowing and all-mighty King of Football Junkies probably doesn't know. A safety occurs when an offensive player commits a foul and the measurement for the penalty starts in the end zone. Or if an offensive player throws an illegal forward pass while standing in the end zone. Throw these examples out at the next football game and watch the food fall out of their mouths.

When points are put on the board as a result of a safety, focus your binoculars on:

➤ The offensive line (offensive players on the field when the safety occurs) getting their butts chewed out for blowing their assignments.

➤ The quarterback as he attempts to walk off the field without any assistance and without letting the bad guys know he has a boo-boo in his head (concussion).

➤ The elated defensive player, who caused the safety, jumping up and down like a kangaroo.

Once the defense has earned the safety, the offense must give up the ball. The official places the ball on the 20-yard line and the ball is kicked to the bad guys (opponents). Bottom line: The offense has turned the ball over to the enemy and has lost the golden opportunity to put points on the board.

2-POINT CONVERSION

After a touchdown, a team can attempt a 2-point conversion or the point after (extra point). A 2-point conversion smells, sounds, and looks just like a touchdown except it is only earned after a touchdown and is worth only 2 points. The 2-point conversion is a calculated ploy to get additional points on the board. The coach will attempt a 2-point conversion when he believes:

➤ The defense can not stop the other team's offense. In these situations, the coach will exploit the defense's inefficiencies and attempt to put 2 points on the board.

➤ The outcome of the game is going to be close enough that the coach feels it is worth attempting a 2-point conversion instead of the extra point. Remember the extra point is worth 1 point while the 2-point conversion puts 2 points on the board.

➤ The kicker is unable to kick the ball between the two uprights. The coach feels that since he knows the kicker is going to miss the uprights he has nothing to lose by attempting the 2-point conversion.

29

➤ The home court advantage is also a factor.

Even in these situations, a coach may not attempt the 2-point conversion if there is not a high probability of success. A failed attempt can demoralize a team. A coach has two primary responsibilities to his team, the organization, and its fans. One is to win, and the other is to build the players' self-esteem. If you believe this, I have some dirt cheap waterfront property in the Mojave Desert to sell you. The coach has only one job, to win. However a winning coach uses various techniques to motivate his players, not tear them down.

POINT AFTER (EXTRA POINT)

Again the point after (extra point) is attempted only after a touchdown. Be careful not to confuse the field goal with the point after. Although both types of points are earned by kicking the football through the uprights, the field goal is worth 3 points and is attempted in lieu of a touchdown.

The point after is awarded to a team when the kicker boots the football between the crossbars (also called "uprights"). The uprights are the two poles that extend vertically from the crossbar. For the point after to count the ball must go between the uprights and over the crossbars. The assemblage of the crossbar and the uprights is called the goal post. With the successful execution of the point after, a team can put 7 points on the board. Mathematically computed that's 1 point for the point after the touchdown and 6points for the touchdown.

As you can see, there are a number of ways for the offense and defense to put points on the board. You might ask yourself, "Then why are the scores so low?" Well if the defense has done its job by stopping the offense from scoring, or if the offense is lousy and cannot score, then theoretically the score should be low. Of course the flip side to this is also true. If the defense cannot stop the offense, the score could be high.

Picture this: On the way to the market (end zone), Mom (quarterback) has to pick up Fran and Otis from football practice. However the coach has made an unexpected decision to keep the guys an additional thirty minutes because he does not like the team's work ethics. Because of this untimely delay, Mom does not have time (only one down remaining) to make it to the market (end zone) and prepare her usual seven-course feast (touchdown). Mom (quarterback) must now look at her alternatives. She can get take-out (punt the ball), go to the market and get dinner on the table as soon as she can (attempt to gain the needed yards for the next series of downs), or go home and make peanut butter and jelly sandwiches (attempt the field goal). Her first choice, getting take-out (punting the ball), costs a little more than making dinner. But at least everyone will be fed at a reasonable hour, leaving her with peace and quiet at the end of the day (keeps the opponent away from the end zone). Her second choice is more cost effective but not very bright as there are going to be some pretty upset family members (fans and organization) if dinner is not served within minutes after they walk in from practice (attempt the needed yards). Her third choice, make peanut butter and jelly sandwich, is a quick and easy answer (puts at least 3 points on the board). Sometimes the sure thing is the best alternative.

To summarize the formula for success is:

TYPE OF SCORE	POINTS EARNED
Touchdown	6 points
Field goal	3 points
Safety	2 points
2-point conversion	2 points
Point after or extra point	1 point

CHAPTER 5

THE OPPORTUNITIES

The offensive team has four opportunities, or "downs," to move the football in order to put points on the board. If the offense is unsuccessful, the opponent has a turn at trying to move the football. Throw in some half-witted rules, male egos, and testosterone, and we have the game of football.

Football sometimes is called a "game of inches." Every inch counts. To earn the next series of downs, you need 10 yards; a yard is thirty-six inches. Therefore you can see, even in football, how each inch is vital; if you cannot make the inches, you're not going to make the yards.

The concept of downs is difficult to understand even for the seasoned football fan. The basic idea is a team has four attempts, or downs, to move the ball 10 yards. The set of downs is referred to as a "series." If a team continues to move the ball at least 10 yards within four downs, then eventually the offense gets closer to the end zone and eventually ends up in the end zone, which means the team has scored a touchdown.

The play called during each down first, second, third, or fourth is similar to the theory behind a successful recipe. Once you successfully complete each step, you get closer to finishing your masterpiece (i.e., successfully moving the ball 10 yards and eventually into the end zone). The four downs as they relate to steps in completing your favorite recipe might include:

> ➤ Making sure you have all the ingredients and supplies.

> ➤ If you do not have all the essentials, begging, borrowing, or buying them from your neighbor.

> ➤ Following the instructions as specified.

➤ Removing the dish from the oven, refrigerator, or work area.

Your strategic approach to getting dinner on the table at a reasonable time (end of game) will dictate your approach to the next task (series of downs). If it is close to dinnertime, (time remaining—one minute) you may pull out all stops and demand that Fran and Otis help in getting dinner on the table. Or you may opt to do it yourself—a quarterback sneak. The touchdown in this situation is when you get to do what you want to do, which could be just watching a good, hard-hitting game of football. Here the final series for that touchdown might include:

➤ Moving the beer from the refrigerator to within inches of your fingertips.

➤ Strategically placing the snacks so all the good stuff is in front of you.

➤ Planting your body on the couch.

➤ Turning on Monday Night Football.

You don't need to go through every task before moving on to the next. It is conceivable to take the beer from the refrigerator, leaving everyone to fend for themselves while you plant your body on the couch so you can watch Monday Night Football (touchdown). The same holds true with football. It is also possible to go from first down to the end zone.

When you hear an official or a fan refer to downs, you normally hear them call out two numbers. The first number is the actual down (attempt) the offense is on—first, second, third, or fourth.

The second number is the number of yards required to reach the magical 10-yard mark and the next set of downs. "First and 10" means the offense is on its first attempt and needs 10 yards for a first down. "Third and 7" means it's the third attempt and the offense has 7 yards to go.

Football is not only a game of inches but also a game of third downs. When a team executes on third downs the team will eventually win. Now what does that mean? It's simple. If the offensive team is successful in moving the ball 10 yards, then they receive another four downs to move the ball another 10 yards. This pattern is repeated over and over until the team scores or until the defensive team is successful in stopping the offense from moving the ball 10 yards. If the defensive team can't stop the offense, it is inevitable that the offense will eventually score.

Let's work through a couple of examples:

- ➤ Chris is thrown a wobbly pass, often called a "duck." However Chris can catch anything because he is my son and he was born to play football. The football is thrown from the 50-yard line. Chris catches the ball and is tackled on the 35-yard line. The ball has effectively been moved 15 yards. By last count 15 yards is greater than 10 yards. Therefore the offense has earned another four attempts or downs to move the ball another 10 yards—or, better yet, into the end zone for the touchdown.

- ➤ On the next attempt (now first and 10), Chris receives the hand-off from the quarterback. With the help of the offensive blockers, Chris artfully outmaneuvers the wide bodies, who attempt to take him down. He successfully gains 9 yards on the play. As a result, the offense needs only 1 yard to earn another set of downs. In football mumbo-jumbo, the next down is called "second and 1." You see, it is not that difficult.

Okay, let's throw a little twist in:

- ➤ My best friend's kid, Mike, catches a 40-yard pass. He does not exhibit the same skills as my son. Although he manages to run for 2 yards, Mike then drops the football and commits the ultimate sin—a fumble, a fumblerooski. The defense recovers the ball. This is commonly referred to as a "turnover." Now the opposing offense takes over and they start on "first and 10."

In football not executing on third downs and turning over the football seals the fate of a game. In other words, it will kill you. Conversely the defense has done its job. It has stopped the offense from moving the ball the necessary 10 yards and has caused a turnover.

Now just when you think you understand the intricacies of downs, there is one exception. When the offense is within 10 yards of the goal line, the situation is referred to as "first and goal." The terminology switch is intended to throw a little excitement into the boring repetitive calls of first and xx, or third and xx, or fourth and inches—no, no, it's "first and goal." Isn't that more exciting? Seriously you can see if a team has been able to successfully move his team within 10 yards of the goal (first and goal) then the probability of putting points on the board dramatically increases and it deserves the enthusiasm of the announcer yelling, "first and goal!"

What happens if the offense cannot move the ball the necessary 10 yards? A seasoned and well-adjusted coach can throw a temper tantrum or maintain his cool discussing the various options and strategies with his offensive coaches. Or conceivably he could do both.

On fourth down, it is essential for the offense to make the touchdown, earn the next set of downs, or get the ball as close to their opponent's end zone as possible. When a team cannot score or earn the next set of downs, the coach can opt for one of the following three choices:

➤ Punt the ball. Here the offense is put in a position of having to move the ball as far as possible before scoring a touchdown. Additionally it eliminates the possibility of giving the bad guys good field position.

➤ Go for it. Attempt to gain the necessary yards for the next series of downs. Here a coach may call a trick play or some kind of fake in an attempt to gain the needed yards. If a team is unsuccessful in executing the necessary yards for the next series of downs, the opposing team's offense takes over where the ball is marked dead.

➤ Attempt the field goal, which, if successful, puts 3 points on the board.

BATTLEFIELD

The field of play, appropriately, is called a football field. The playing field is 100 yards long and most stupid men remember the field being 50 feet wide. However the field is actually 53 and 1/3 yards-wide. Be prepared to correct the big lug on the width of field next time he brings it up. The field is marked off in 5-yard increments starting from goal line up to the 50-yard line, which is the center of field. The field is divided into two halves; each half has 50 yards. With the field marked off in 5-yard increments, it is easy to keep track of how many yards the offense has moved the ball and how many yards are needed to earn the next series of downs.

If you can count, you can keep track of the yards. If you cannot count, watch the chain gang. Whatever you do, do not ask the football junkie sitting next to you, "How many yards do we need?" Start demonstrating your newfound football expertise. Make bold statements such as "Man, only 3 yards for a first down," or "No way, we still need 11 yards for a touchdown, we better punt." Don't be afraid to make a mistake. Otherwise, it will take you longer to get the hang of the football lingo.

You may also notice in addition to the field markings there is an area on the sidelines where the coaches and players stand. This area is commonly referred to as the box. Coaches and players are required to stay in this designated area. The box extends to both the 35-yard lines and is really not a box and in many cases is not even marked off. In professional ball, where the owners can splurge and buy non-essential extravagances, the area is covered with a tarp. In college and high school football, where money is scarce, the area is not covered. The box is intended to keep the coaches and players separated from the officials and other players on the field, which, it is hoped, will thwart the coaches from running onto the field and killing either the player who screwed up or the official who made that horrendous call. However in reality the box serves no purpose when all mayhem breaks loose. The yellow tape at a crime scene is similar to the box. Should you cross it, you can expect to be removed from the area or receive a verbal tongue-lashing and/or a citation.

Standing in front of the play, you may notice three guys holding a long stick and wearing a luminous colored vest. These guys are members of the infamous chain gang. They are not criminals doing community service; they are actually three sensitive and caring individuals, of any size, color, height, or for that matter sex. The brightly colored vest is worn so they stand out and, they hope, avoid getting run over by an overzealous player. You have to be blind to miss the gang. After all how many guys wear an orange vest, and walk around with an eight-foot stick, or for that matter, stand smack in front of a play?

The technical name for the sticks held by the chain gang are called measuring sticks (like a measuring cup). The two chain gang members holding the measuring sticks are referred to as rod men (ooh, so wicked). What you might not see is the 10-yard chain attached to the bottom of each stick. (Sort of like the chains criminals wear around their feet.) When the official calls for a measurement, the rod men run onto the field. They place one of the sticks at the spot where the series of downs started. They then stretch the other stick 10 yards. If the ball is within the two sticks then the offense did not move the ball 10 yards. If any part of the ball is outside of the sticks then the team "executed" and advances to the next down. See the similarity between the measuring cup and the measuring sticks?

The third member of the chain gang holds the down marker. The down marker displays the number of the down a team is playing. After each possession he advances the down card from 1 to 2, or 2 to 3, or 3 to 4; he then positions himself at the line of scrimmage ready and eager for the next play.

CHAPTER 6

THE KEEPERS

Girlfriends, this chapter is extremely important. Try not to mess this up. Nothing makes a person, female or for that matter even a male, look more foolish than not knowing the proper name of the official. It is pathetic to hear someone yell at the referee when they should be yelling at the umpire or vice versa. Yelling at the wrong official shows complete ignorance. Men love this; its gives them a sense of supcriority.

The officials are the keepers of the rules, including the responsibility of placing or spotting the football at the exact place where the play has ended. At times the ball may be under the heap of players on the field. Or the official may not be in position to see where the play ended. In these cases, the official, with a great sense of confidence, jogs over to the spot where he "thinks" the ball was downed. Never mind that the official's guesswork could cost a team the chance to put the ball in the end zone or, even worse, a win. So much for the "game of inches."

Depending on whether you are winning or losing, the officials seem to exhibit numerous deficiencies. Accordingly officials become the targets of the frustration of fans and coaches. The primary complaint is inconsistency. Some officials exercise a loose interpretation of the rules while others cannot separate their personal shortcomings and frustrations from their professional job. A secondary complaint is because officiating is only a part-time job, the quality and consistency that you might get from a full-timer isn't there. However, since football has never utilized officials in a full-time capacity, we don't know if this would work either. This argument, full versus part-time officials, could just be another excuse for what really is crummy officiating.

Officials run in packs, marking their area and punishing any player who dares to cross the line. In professional ball, officials work with the same officials. They travel, eat, but don't sleep together. This methodology allows each official to understand the other officials' strengths and weaknesses, thus allowing them to adjust their officiating style to compensate for their fellow team member. Contrary to professional ball, the officials used in high school and playoff games do not work as part of the same team. On occasion this presents problems, as each official does not know the other officials' inefficiencies. Therefore they do not adjust their officiating style, and consequently you see some really horrendous calls.

Even though it would seem that officials have a slightly higher intelligence than the average football player, the truth is these guys are just like the rest. Once they get on the field, the testosterone takes over and they feel the need to leave their mark on the game by making as many calls as possible. For example, have you ever seen when a play is over and the teams are running off the field? If one of the players does not get completely off the field, even if that player does not have anything to do with the play, that's a penalty—too many men on the field. This is a stupid penalty. But the official will always call it anyway, even if it has nothing to do with the play going on, because he needs to prove he is the man in charge. Ooh, baby, we love a man who thinks he's in charge.

The football game is controlled by a crew of seven gentlemen called the **referee, umpire, head linesman, field judge, side judge, line judge**, and **back judge**.

REFEREE

The referee is the head honcho on the field and is responsible for running the game and for penalty administration. He has the last word in disputes that arise from scoring, downs, or any other calls not covered by one of the other officials. The referee stands in the offensive backfield (behind the offensive players), which enables him to watch for:

➤ Holding fouls (offensive linemen holds or grabs any part of a defender's body or uniform);

➤ Illegal motion (offensive player moves any part of his body before the ball is snapped);

➤ Watches for roughing the quarterback (illegal contact after the quarterback has thrown the ball);

➤ Watches for roughing the kicker (illegal contact after the kicker has booted the ball);

➤ Watches for the backward pass (pass to a player running behind the player with the ball).

Because he is the head guy he is also responsible for:

➤ Placing the ball at the spot where the next play will begin;

➤ Signaling the start of play by blowing his whistle;

➤ Signaling the operator to start the play clock so he can keep track of how much time a team takes between plays;

➤ Making announcements;

➤ Giving the appropriate hand signals and/or using the field mike;

➤ Notifying each team about time-outs;

➤ Waving on the chain gang to take the measurement to see if a team has made the next series of downs;

➤ Providing team captains and coaches details of the foul and offering the team captain of the non-offending team the option of accepting or declining the penalty.

UMPIRE

The umpire stands in the defensive backfield. He is responsible for:

➤ Checking the equipment (like keeping the ball dry);

➤ Keeping the game moving;

➤ Ensuring good sportsmanship;

➤ Officially watching the clock;

➤ Watching players on the line of scrimmage for false starts (player moving before start of play);

➤ Watching for ineligible linemen downfield (offensive lineman, moves past the line of scrimmage before the ball is snapped);

➤ Watching for holding.

HEAD LINESMAN

The head linesman is positioned on the line of scrimmage. Well, not exactly on the line; after all you do not want to see these guys standing smack in the middle of the play. Never mind they might get hurt, more importantly they might block our view. They actually position themselves down the line. He watches for:

➤ The offsides (players crossing into the neutral zone);

➤ When the ball goes out of bounds;

➤ Supervises the chain gang;

➤ Pass interference on his side of the field;

➤ Works with the line judge and signals the touchdown on goal line plays.

LINE JUDGE

The line judge stands on the opposite side of the field from the head linesman. He watches for the same things as the head linesman except he watches only for those infractions that occur on his side of the field. He is also the referee's helper in calling penalties at the line and on his side of the field. The line judge will:

➤ Make sure the quarterback does not cross the line of scrimmage;

➤ Watch for the backward and lateral pass;

➤ Mark the spot where the ball goes out of bounds;

➤ Oversee the timing of the game;

➤ Time the intermission;

➤ Get the honor of firing a blank pistol to start each period;

➤ Carry a clock in his pocket, just in case the official clock breaks.

BACK JUDGE AND SIDE JUDGE

The back judge and side judge are positioned behind the defense. The back judge stands behind the line judge while the side judge positions himself behind the head linesman. With the exception of field goal duties, the back judge and side judge:

- Watch for the illegal hold on the deep pass;

- Ensure the correct numbers of players are on the field;

- Work with the field judge on signaling field goals;

- Watch for clipping on the long runs (hitting a defender below the waist from behind);

- Watch for players in the back field who make the unfortunate blunder of going out of bounds;

- Watch for movement from the offensive line.

FIELD JUDGE

The field judge is the last guy in the defense's territory. Because he is all by his lonesome, he is in the best position to watch for infractions that occur in the backfield and that are out of sight from the other officials. These include:

- Covering the deep punt, the deep pass, and pass interference;

- Timing the count for punting the ball (the ball must be punted within thirty seconds);

- Timing the halftime break and time-outs;

- Ruling with the back judge on field goals and the point after attempt.

Every time you've seen a field goal or the point after attempt, you have watched the field judge and back judge run and stand on each side of the goal post. Depending on if the kick was successful they will extend their arms straight in the air. For an unsuccessful kick they will wave it off, by swinging both arms in a lateral movement.

41

The outfits worn by the officials, otherwise known as uniforms, are sanctioned by the top football mucky-mucks. The uniforms include polyester pants in the color white, a polyester shirt with horizontally black and white stripes, a coordinating black belt, black cleats, and a baseball-type cap. These guys cannot be mistaken for the real beef on the field. Not only are they fewer in number, but they are smaller in stature.

All of the officials are dressed the same except for the referee, who gets to sport a white baseball cap. Everyone then knows he is the head guy on the field (it's a macho thing). The other officials have to wear black caps. The letters designating the official's position may be placed on the front and back of each official's shirt.

Each official keeps a yellow flag in his rear right pocket or between his belt and his pants. The base of the yellow flag is filled with weights so when it is thrown it can be thrown in the vicinity of the play. Here's the sequence: The official observes the infraction then grabs and throws the yellow flag in the general vicinity of where the penalty occurred.

After an official throws a yellow flag, all of the officials meet to agree on the infraction. The officials' conference presents a united front to the coaches, players, and fans. This is the "team approach" to officiating. Once the officials have conferred, the referee uses hand signals and his field mike to inform coaches, players, and fans of the infraction, penalty, and sometimes the number of the player who caused the infraction. The field mike is essential for those men who pretend to know all the rules of the game, but who in fact may know only the basics. If the officials used only hand signals, think of how dumb some men might look, especially when asked, "What was that for?" or "What does that mean?"

Infractions are frequently called before a play even starts. If the infraction is flagrant, all of the officials may even throw their yellow flags. This is a beautiful sight, especially when the infraction is against the bad guys. Even though a flag has been thrown, the play continues until a whistle is blown. Only after the whistle is blown are players required to stop playing. However, this does not preclude players from getting in as many cheap shots as they can.

Cheap shots are common when players are part of the pile of meat on the field. Since officials cannot see what goes on underneath the pile, players will get in as many cheap shots as they can. Now you may ask yourself, why would nice boys do this? The answer is simple: possession of the ball. Players will do whatever it takes to get the player to release the ball. Common cheap shots include biting, pinching, slugging, spitting, hair pulling, or poking the old eyeballs.

CHAPTER 7

BROKEN RULES AND PUNISHMENTS

Infractions are the rules of the game that are broken. The penalty is the punishment. In football the player committing the infraction may cause his team a 5-yard, 10-yard, or 15-yard penalty, or a loss of down. In addition the player may find himself getting thrown out of the game (evicted), receiving a personal fine, or any combination of these. This is not a good thing.

The severity of the penalty depends on the infraction. In real life, the severity of a penalty is similar to:

➣ 5-yard penalty: Small mistake. Similar to when a kid forgets to take the trash out, mow the yard, or make their bed. Penalty: Send the kid to their room.

➣ 10-yard penalty: Medium mistake. Like when the significant other forgets to mention he invited his mother to dinner. Penalty: Don't let him know ahead of time when your mother is coming over for dinner.

➣ 15-yard penalty: Big mistake. OOPS, when a boyfriend or hubby forgets your birthday or anniversary. Penalty: Buy yourself a really expensive gift with his money.

➣ Loss of Down: Depending on when the loss of down occurs it can either be a catastrophic mistake or just a big mistake. A catastrophic mistake occurs when time is running out and you need every down. For example, if you lose your credit card a week before Christmas. A big mistake occurs during the course of the game, such as not being able to use your credit card for your next purchase.

Football for Females

It really is easy, except the mucky-mucks have illogical and complicated terms for what could have been a very simple and logical game. In an attempt to make the game more friendly, why not use adjectives to describe the severity of the infraction? An unintentional foul (5 yards) could be called a "goof." An intentional foul (10 yards) could be called a "bungle." A personal violation a "screw up," and a loss of downs a "blunder."

Rather than saying "penalty," how about "the punishment is?" Perhaps someone should have taken the thesaurus away from these literary geniuses. After all we are talking about a game—a game meant for entertaining millions. Forget about the fact that this sport is also the bread and butter for owners, advertisers, coaches, and players. Okay, maybe "penalty" isn't that harsh.

Following is a table of the major infractions, the team (offense or defense) likely to cause the foul, the penalties likely to be imposed, the effect of such penalty, and where the penalty is assessed:

INFRACTION	PENALTY Team committing foul	ENFORCEMENT SPOT Effect on down
Fouls Occurring at the Start of a play		
Delay of game (play clock expires before the start of the next play).	Loss of 5 yards. Offensive foul.	Line of scrimmage. Repeat down.
Encroachment (if any player other than the center moves and then has physical contact with a player prior to the snap).	Loss of 5 yards. Offensive or defensive foul.	Line of scrimmage. Repeat down.
Failure to wear proper equipment (i.e. not wearing a mouthpiece).	Loss of 5 yards. Offensive/defensive foul.	Previous spot.
False Start (moving prematurely).	Loss of 5 yards. Offensive foul.	Line of Scrimmage. Repeat down
Illegal formation (players not lined up correctly on the field).	Loss of 5 yards. Offensive foul.	Previous spot. Repeat down.

INFRACTION	PENALTY **Team committing foul**	ENFORCEMENT SPOT **Effect on down**
Illegal motion (an offensive player is moving any part of his body when the ball is snapped. Exception: 1 offensive player in the backfield).	Loss of 5 yards. Offensive foul.	Previous spot. Repeat down.
Offsides (a player other than the center is moving any part of his body prior to when the ball is snapped).	Loss of 5 yards. Offensive or defensive foul.	Previous spot. Repeat down.
Too many men on the field (a team has more than 11 players on the field).	Loss of 5 yards. Offensive or defensive foul.	Previous spot. Repeat down.
Fouls Occurring During a Play		
Facemask (accidentally grabbing bars in front of facemask).	Loss of 5 yards Offensive or defensive foul	Spot varies. Repeat down.
Holding (showing sign of endearment at in ap propriate time).	Offensive foul—Loss of 10 yards. Defensive foul—Loss of 50 yards.	Spot varies. Repeat down.
Illegal forward pass (thrown from beyond the line of scrimmage).	Loss of 5 yards. Offensive foul.	Spot of pass. Loss of down.
Illegal forward pass to an ineligible receiver.	Loss of 10 yards. Offensive foul.	Previous spot. Repeat down.

INFRACTION	PENALTY **Team committing foul**	ENFORCEMENT SPOT **Effect on down**
Illegal use of hands (offensive player tries to help his teammate by pushing him forward with his hands or uses his hands to contact the opponent's neck, face, or head).	Loss of 5 yards. Defensive foul.	Spot varies. Automatic first down.
Illegal use of hands (defensive player pushes a pass receiver who is more than 5 yards from the line of scrimmage or a defensive player shoves his hands forward to contact an opponent's neck, face, or head).	Loss of 10 yards. Offensive foul.	Spot varies. Repeat down.
Ineligible member of kicking team downfield (on a kicking play, a player on the kicking team crosses the line of scrimmage before the ball is kicked).	Loss of 5 yards. Offensive foul.	Previous spot. Repeat down.
Ineligible receiver downfield (player who has tried to cheat by running ahead of the pack).	Loss of 5 yards. Offensive foul.	Previous spot. Repeat down.
Intentional grounding (getting rid of the football before the quarterback gets sacked).	Loss of 10 yards. Offensive foul.	Previous spot. Spot of foul. Loss of down.

INFRACTION	PENALTY **Team committing foul**	ENFORCEMENT SPOT **Effect on down**
Pass interference (a player prevents an opponent from catching a pass prior to the ball's arrival).	Defensive foul.	Spot of foul. Automatic first down.
Pass interference (same as above only the offense is attempting to stop the defense from intercepting the pass).	Loss of 10 yards. Offensive foul.	Previous spot. Repeat down.
Running into the kicker (if a defensive player, while trying to block the ball, runs into a punter or place-kicker).	Loss of 5 yards. Loss of 15-yards (flagrant). Defensive foul.	Previous spot. Repeat down.
Personal fouls Occurring During Play		
Chop block or illegal cut (if an offensive player blocks a defensive player below the waist while the latter is already being blocked).	Loss of 15 yards. Offensive foul.	Spot varies. Repeat down.
Clipping (blocking a player below the waist from behind).	Loss of 15 yards. Offensive or defensive foul.	Spot varies. Automatic first down.
Facemask (intentionally twisting or pulling the opponent's facemask).	Loss 15 yards. Offensive or defensive foul.	Spot varies. Automatic first down.

INFRACTION	PENALTY **Team committing foul**	ENFORCEMENT SPOT **Effect on down**
Illegal block below the waist (when player blocks an opponent below the waist during a runback after a kickoff, punt, safety kick, fumble recovery or interception).	Loss of 15 yards. Offensive or defensive foul.	Spot varies. Automatic first down.
Roughing the kicker (intentional, defender not only runs into kicker but also hits him hard).	Loss of 15 yards. Defensive foul.	Spot varies. Automatic first down.
Roughing the passer (if a defensive player runs into the passer after the ball has left the passer's hand or intentionally tries to harm him).	Loss of 15 yards. Defensive foul.	Spot varies. Automatic first down.
Striking, kicking, kneeling or intentionally contacting an official (you can figure this one out).	Loss of 15 yards and ejection from the game. Offensive or defensive foul.	From where play stopped.
Unsportsmanlike conduct (when a player does not act in the spirit of the game of football, including nasty words, taunting, or celebrating too hard in front of the opponent).	Loss of 15 yards Offensive or defensive foul.	Succeeding spot. Automatic first down.

Understanding the infractions is a must. If you don't the game seems to drag on forever. Once you do understand, recognizing the infraction and calling it out is fun.

I remember during one of the many games watched at our house I was in the kitchen with my friend, Susie. Like any real football fan I have a television in my kitchen so I don't miss a thing. During one particular play, the quarterback threw the ball to his favorite target (receiver). The ball was tipped high into the air by one of the defensive lineman. Before the intended receiver could catch the ball, the defensive end tipped the ball and then flattened him. As Susie and I placed raw meat on a serving tray, I heard someone yell, "That's pass interference!" I turned to Susie and said loudly for the guys to over hear, "That's not pass interference. The lineman tipped the ball, it's a live ball, baby." No pass interference; I turned to Susie and started chuckling. We heard the guys whisper, "Can you believe that #!@#?"

CHAPTER 8

IT'S PLAYTIME

Though the game seems to last forever, playing time for a professional game is actually only sixty minutes, a high school game only forty-eight minutes. The basic game is comprised of four quarters—two quarters per half. A professional quarter is fifteen minutes while a high school quarter is only twelve minutes. However, once you throw in a few injury time-outs, television time-outs, and coaching time-outs, the game seems to last forever.

Each team is allowed six time-outs, three per half. If the time-outs are not used, the coach cannot carry them over to use in the next half or in overtime. A team cannot call consecutive time-outs; a play must be run between the time-outs. In professional ball, two time-outs are available during overtime. College ball only allows one time-out.

Once the official acknowledges a player's request for a time-out, the officials charges the time-out to that player's team. The ball is then dead and play cannot resume until the time-out has expired. With the exception of the last two minutes of the game, a time-out cannot exceed one minute and fifty seconds. A time-out called in the last two minutes of the game lasts only forty seconds; time is of the essence. These players have things to do, places to go, beer to guzzle, and women to chase. The official declares a live ball within twenty-five seconds after the time-out has expired. If an official needs additional time, he may call another time-out. An official's time-out is not charged to either team.

Once a team has used its allotted time-outs, they are out of luck should their team get in a pickle. The coach cannot stop the clock to discuss the next series of plays with his players. In this case, the quarterback needs to act decisively and intelligently. If this doesn't work he can always look over at the sidelines and watch for hand signals, or listen to the little voices in his helmet (microphone in helmet). Here's why time-out management is so important. As the song goes, "Time is on our side," but this is not true when it comes to the game of football. But it is hoped the players can put their testosterone on the shelf and attack the situation logically.

Once a team has used all of its time-outs, the only time the clock stops is:

➤ For an injured player. A clever and cagey player used to be able to fake the time-out to stop the clock. However the "rules committee" finally figured it out. Now if a player gets hurt in the last two minutes of the game, the clock is stopped, the injured player is rolled off the field and the official then adds ten seconds to the play clock.

➤ When the ball goes out of bounds, the heads-up players attempt to get the ball out of bounds before the ball is whistled dead. When the quarterback is trying to manage the time remaining you will see him throw the football close to the side lines so the receiver can get out of bounds more easily.

➤ When time is required to repair damaged equipment.

➤ To reset the chains after a team has successfully moved the ball 10 yards for a first down.

➤ When there are two minutes left on the clock. The two-minute warning alerts both teams to get their act together, stop goofing off, and start playing some serious football. The two-minute warning is also an indicator that the game could last anywhere from two to forty-five more minutes.

The entire concept of time-outs is similar to the allotted cooking times specified in recipes. Once time has elapsed on the timer (official clock), you cannot allocate that time to another recipe (second half or in overtime). The bread has already started to rise, baby. When time has elapsed on the buzzer your choices are simple:

➤ If the food is not done, try to stop the clock (injury time-out).

➤ If the food looks and smells horrible, throw it away, order a pizza, and let everyone know the food must have been rotten (attempt to get the ball out of bounds).

➤ When the timer goes off and you realize you forgot to turn the oven on (repair broken equipment), start the timer again.

➤ When the timer goes off, you check the food and you realize the oven must not be correctly calibrated (reset the time after a team earns the next set of downs).

➤ Take the food out of the oven (time expired) and serve the dish raw. Tell everyone the recipe calls for the dish to be served that way.

If, at the end of the game, the score is tied, the tie maybe resolved in overtime. This, however, depends on the level of play. For example:

➤ Professional Ball: The teams play an additional fifteen minutes or until one team scores. The first team to score is declared the winner, and that's it folks, the game is over. This is commonly referred to as "sudden death overtime." Prior to starting overtime, each team is given three minutes to catch their breath, to strategize, and to refocus. The coin toss is again used to determine which team will receive or defend. With the exception of playoff games, if during the fifteen-minute overtime a team has not scored, then the game ends in a tie. During the playoffs, an additional fifteen minutes are played until one team has more points on the board than the other team. A playoff game cannot end in a tie since there must be a winner to advance to the next round.

➤ College: Prior to 1996, if a game ended in a tie, well, the game ended in a tie. In 1996, this all changed. Now there must be a winner. Each extra period consists of one offensive possession for each team. The possession starts on the opponent's 25-yard line. Each offensive team is given a chance to score a touchdown or a field goal. The offensive team has four downs to score a touchdown or a field goal. If the score is still tied after its third attempt, each team is forced to attempt the 2-point conversion rather than the extra point.

➤ High school: During an overtime period each team has an opportunity for an offensive series of downs. There is a three-minute intermission between the end of the fourth quarter and the start of overtime. If the score still remains tied after the three-minute period then the procedure is repeated until one team ends up with more points then the other. If a safety is scored, the ball is placed on the 10-yard line in possession of the team that was on defense.

THE BALL

The game of football is played with an inflated ball called (you guessed it) a football. Made out of pigskin with an inflated rubber balloon inside, it is shaped like a blimp and must be pumped up to an exact weight and length. White laces decorate the outer skin of the football and also provide a nice dash of color to a tightly thrown spiral. In addition the laces serve to give the players something to grip.

The start of each play is played with a dry football. The football can get wet from the weather or from the sweaty hands of the players. The quarterback keeps a towel draped from the front of his pants for two reasons. One is to look cool, and the other is to towel off his hands. The official may also have his own towel to dry off the football. When the towel does not work, he can request a clean ball from the official. In profession ball, teams are allowed to use thirty-six balls in a game; that is eighteen footballs per half. Conceivably after each play the center can request a dry ball from the official. The official may grant or refuse the request.

PLAYERS' ARMORY

The most important pieces of football equipment are the protective pads. After all who in their right mind would collide with a locomotive traveling thirty-five miles per hour unless he is properly equipped? Except of course for maybe Lyle Alzado (former Oakland Raider, lineman), Mean Joe Green (former Pittsburgh Steeler lineman), or Dick Butkus (former Chicago Bears linebacker).

The protective equipment includes a helmet, facemask, shoulder pads, rib pads, hip pads, thigh pads, knee pads, and, most important, the cup. The right equipment can protect one's ability to, walk, run, father children, and remember who and where one is.

If the helmet is not on the player's head, you will see it either strapped to the back of his pants or carried by the player. This is not because the helmet is regarded as a security blanket. Instead a player, coach, or official running downfield could trip on the helmet.

Again do not worry about proper equipment. We will leave it up to the coaching staff and the officials to ensure the big boys are outfitted properly.

CHAPTER 9

LET THE GAMES BEGIN!

When both teams charge onto their respective sides of the field, you know it is game time. Watching a game of football can be fun, rousing, and exhilarating when you are properly prepared. Preparation, of course, depends on whether you are watching a game in front of the tube or out in the open air.

HINTS FOR WATCHING AN INSIDE GAME

Not all football games are watched in the fresh air. You can also sit in the privacy of your home where no one can see that you have become a closet football junkie. You can watch live games, reruns, highlights, or taped games.

Taped? Let us not forget Proud Papa. He is going to tape the games and replay them every chance he can. He will watch it by himself. He will make you watch it with him. He'll watch it again when friends come over, pointing out moments in which his son does something fantastic or almost makes the play.

This is why preparation is critical. If you are properly prepared, enduring the three hours or so of a football game will be doable. Rest assured: By the time you are done with this book you will be properly equipped to sit and enjoy the game, thus enabling you to spend real quality time watching a football game with him.

Preparation includes moving everything in the vicinity out of the way where the big boys will be watching the game. Otherwise don't get upset when things are chipped or broken when the game is brought live into your home. But more importantly, preparation includes having enough food to feed the bottomless pits who may be hovering around the television or who have worked up an appetite reenacting a previous play. The following works at any level of play:

➤ Beverages: Preferable clear sodas, so when they spill it won't show on your carpet. Or if they do, have the club soda ready. Be sure to have some bottled water, beer, and ice--not only for the drinks but to keep the hot heads cool.

➤ Appetizers: Brainless Wonder Dip: Go to the store and buy packaged dip mix. Scoop out contents and serve in a plastic container. Don't go to the trouble of making something special. The well-mannered gents will be so engrossed in the game they won't even notice what is served. In this situation, quantity counts, not quality.

➤ Bean Dip: On second thought, forget this recipe. Although, in case of a power outage, the benefit of having enjoyed the bean dip could be used to provide bursts of light and heat.

➤ Snacks: An assortment of fruit, sliced in small bites to minimize the possibility of someone choking. Meat and bread, real food for the real man, right.

➤ Weenie in a bun: Barbecue a hot dog until it has curled or exploded. Top with mustard, mayonnaise, onions, pickles, and chili till it oozes all over.

➤ Paper products: You certainly don't want to get stuck cleaning up after everyone has left or have dishes broken when the armchair quarterback sets out to practice his favorite pass play. The following items are essential:

  • Napkins—So they don't use the edge of the couch or their shirt sleeves.

  • Paper plates—So they don't use the palm of their hand to eat out of.

  • Paper cups—So maybe they will get the hint all by themselves not to drink from the container.

Preparing and eating snacks helps to relieve the agony of watching the players, coaches, officials, and any other football fan in the vicinity acting like children or generally acting like a pack of prehistoric animals. You also should not have any misconceptions that the lugs in front of the television are going to be polite company or interesting conversationalists. The only thing these guys are going to be talking about is football, football, and, oh yeah, football. Rest assured it does not take long to pick up on the crude and primitive communicating signals:

> ➤ Crushing a can against the forehead: "I'd like another drink."

> ➤ Wiping his face on his shirt: "I'd get a napkin but I might miss something."

> ➤ Picking up the plate and licking it: "Is there any more food?"

> ➤ Farting: "I'm ready for dessert."

> ➤ Belching: "Thank you."

HINTS FOR WATCHING AN OUTSIDE GAME

> ➤ Be sure to bring a fanny cushion, butt warmer, or anything else comfortable to sit on. Otherwise, after having planted your buttocks on those bleachers for three hours, you will definitely have a sore rump.

> ➤ Nothing is worse than watching a game while you're freezing. So even if the game is in the early afternoon, bring a blanket. For evening games, gloves, a hat, and a muffler are a must.

> ➤ For day games, sun lotion, sun block, and even an umbrella are essential. It may seem silly, but it will save you from the sun's blistering rays and an evening of excruciating pain.

> ➤ You may or may not need binoculars, depending on the size of the stadium. But again be prepared. You could end up watching a crummy game. In this case, you can use the binoculars as a diversion. Use them to people-watch, watch the coach's theatrical performances, or get a close-up of the players yelling or celebrating with each other. The options are endless.

LET THE GAMES BEGIN

Now that we are prepared for the type of game we will be watching, we are now ready for the battle of the brawn to commence. Oops, not quite! The national anthem must be sung. For one to earn the honor of singing the national anthem, the inability to hit the notes goes a long way. Usually listening to the national anthem causes the same physical reaction as listening to someone running a fingernail down a chalkboard. The body quivers and shakes, causing an immediate case of goose bumps.

After the national anthem and prior to the start of the game, the team captains participate in a crude ritual called the "coin toss." With today's high-tech environment, you would think football mucky-mucks could come up with a more state-of-the-art process for starting a game. But change is difficult, even in the game of football, so we still have the old coin toss ritual. The official conducts this ritual in the middle of the field. The official tosses a two-sided coin into the air. The official then asks the captains from the visiting team to call heads or tails, hence the "coin toss." You've got to love these guys. They are so clever with their phraseology.

The coin toss gives the team captains an opportunity to discuss like gentleman which team will receive the football, which team will kick the football, and the direction the football will be kicked.

Seasoned coaches have strategies for everything, including the coin toss. That's why coaches would not allow team captains to make the monumental decision of "to receive or not to receive" all by themselves.

Coaches evaluate everything that could possibly affect the outcome of the game, including the benefits of kicking or receiving the ball at the start of the game versus waiting until the second half to receive or kick the ball. Coaches know everything, including how to predict the weather, analyze the wind direction at the start of the game, and the possible wind shifts during the game. Will it be more advantageous to kick the ball at the start of the game? What are the chances the wind will die down by halftime? Or will the entire game end up as "Gone with the Wind?" The coach may elect to go against the wind in the first half in order to go with the wind in the second half. Going with the wind supposedly gives a team an advantage.

Then again some coaches just like to start on defense or on offense in order to establish the tempo of the game.

Hence when the visiting team wins the coin toss, the coach will have instructed the team captains whether their team is going to receive or kick the football.

After the coin toss, the official turns, faces the receiving team, blows his whistle, and moves his arms in a three-quarters circular movement. This dramatic performance signals to the coaches that it is time to bring their warriors to the battlefield.

In addition to pretending they have made the decision to receive or kick the ball, team captains do have other real responsibilities, including:

➢ Discussing penalties with the official—that is after His Majesty, the official, has called the team captains back on the field for the discussion.

➢ Leading and inspiring the team. Keep in mind, any player can be a leader. A true leader doesn't need the title to take a leadership role. Any player can assume the role.

CHAPTER 10

THE HERD (Types of Teams)

The game of football requires savvy coaches to match and maximize the talent on their team against the competition's talent. A coach, if he wants to win, will put the team's best pass blockers on the left side in order to protect his right-handed quarterback.

Players are considered either skilled or non-skilled players. Skilled players are often considered the "pretty boys" of the team—they love the glory, jewelry, and flashy clothes. They may go so far as to change their dirty uniforms at halftime so they always look clean and pretty. The non-skilled players are the true "hogs" of the game. They don't care what they look like, they just love the game, the competition, and the physical contact. The non-skilled players are the heart and soul of the team.

Each football squad has three teams: offense, defense, and special teams. Only one team from each side is allowed on the field at any time. The officials' job is to maintain order, including ensuring that only one team is on the field at a time. Otherwise you would have mass havoc on the field.

Keeping track of Fran, Otis, and Ollie including what time they'll be home, who they are with, or how they're getting home is more complicated than the officials' job of merely counting the number of players on the field. When a team does botch up and has too many players on the field, the official will penalize that team.

The starting squad is made up of twenty-two players, eleven defensive players who are used to keep the opposing offense from putting points on the board and eleven offensive players whose job is to put points on the board. These twenty-two players are called "starters." The second and third string players complement the starters and are also an integral part of the team.

A player's responsibilities to the team are comparable to that of a family member and their responsibilities to the entire family. The Bank family (squad) includes Tony (coach), Mom (management), Fran, (offensive player), Otis, (defensive player), and Ollie (kicker). Each member of the family is equally important to Mr. and Mrs. Bank. In addition each sibling has a responsibility to each other (teammates), friends (fans), and society (league). Nothing less is acceptable.

Of the eleven players on the offensive team, at least seven players must be on the line of scrimmage. Typically you do not find the quarterback, running backs, or receivers on the line of scrimmage. These individuals, considered skill players, are stationed in the middle of the field for their own protection. Accordingly you find the "hogs" taking the brunt of the defense's punishment. Then, when they think the coast is clear, they come out from the backfield and run the ball in for the glory.

Football is a team sport, and every player must contribute to the team's success, even the water boy. There is no "I" in the spelling of team. The quarterback, running back, and receiver really cannot stand around in the backfield until the coast is clear. Occasionally they too have to get a little dirty in the effort to move the ball.

It should come as no surprise that even the arbitrary use of numbers is a no-no. Accordingly each player, depending on his position, is assigned a jersey with a number from 1 through 99. It is not good enough to have the players wear any unique number; they actually wear a number depending on their position. For example, five of the seven players on the line of scrimmage must be numbered between 50 to 79. Clearly there must be some deep-rooted logic for this seemingly ridiculous rule.

Players on the same team cannot wear the same number nor can they be on the field at the same time.

The table below shows the series of numbers you might see on players' jerseys:

OFFENSIVE TEAM	JERSEY NUMBER
Quarterback, Punter, & Place Kicker	1 through 19
Running Back	20 through 49
Center	50 through 50 or 60 through 79, if needed
Guard	60 through 69
Tackle	70 through 79
Wide receiver & Tight End	80 through 89
DEFENSIVE TEAM	
Lineman	60 through 79 or 90 through 99, if needed
Back	20 through 49
Linebackers	50 through 59 or 90 through 99, if needed
End	80 through 89

CHAPTER 11

THE FLOCK (Offense)

A strong offense consistently moves the ball downfield and earns first downs. If the offensive team does not move the ball and continually turns the ball over, you have either a lousy team or a coach who is not playing André in the right position. The easiest thing to do is blame the coach, the lack of talent, or the crummy officiating.

Players are responsible for positioning themselves correctly on the field. In football lingo, that means doing what you are told to do. For example, knocking opponents down to make the "holes" or the "pockets" so the little guy with the ball can run through. Some coaches use tactics such as fear, verbal abuse, and threats to motivate and make sure players position themselves correctly on the field. Because players love the game and have grown accustomed to these motivational techniques, they accept it has the norm.

Proper positioning results in:

➤ The quarterback getting good protection (not condoms) so he can execute the play.

➤ The receiver being in the right place and the defense in the wrong place.

➤ The offensive linemen attacking the defensive rushers.

➤ The quarterbacks having no excuse for making a lousy throw.

The offensive plans and strategies are designed to confuse the defense so the offense can move the ball downfield and score. A good offense needs only seconds to move the ball. Therefore it is imperative that a good offensive player is fast and a defensive player is strong enough to stop any offensive effort. Many of the offensive players can run a 40-yard dash in under five seconds.

OFFENSIVE POSITIONS AND RESPONSIBILITIES

The **quarterback** positions himself behind the center. When the ball is placed on the ground, the quarterback places his hands underneath the center's rump where they remain until the center hikes the ball. This is one of the more absurd stances of the game. What is the quarterback doing with his hands under there? Why is he the only guy who gets to keep his hands clean and warm before the play starts?

The offensive line cannot move once the quarterback puts his hands under the center and yells, "Ready, set!" The ends and backs can move as long as they are not on the line of scrimmage—but not at the same time. Only one offensive player can be "in motion."

The quarterback's mission is to lead and inspire the team to a "W" (win). He is in charge of the team on the field. He calls the plays in the huddle, yells out the signals, and receives the snap from the center.

My son, Rob, exhibits many of the attributes a coach should have. He's good looking, smart, intelligent, and understands the game of football. When the neighborhood kids come over for a game of street football, Rob oversees the selection of the teams. First, he selects Chris for quarterback of the winning team. He knows Chris will call the right play. He knows Chris won't call a quarterback sneak when it is "second and 15." Rob also knows Chris can accurately throw the football and can control the other kids in the neighborhood (offensive team). The neighborhood kids also respect Chris, which is why they are very willing to follow his lead.

Once the quarterback receives the football, he can pass the ball forward, backward, or sideways. However he can only pass the ball forward if he is behind the line of scrimmage. At first semblance this appears to be another feeble-witted football rule. After all why can't the quarterback throw the ball from beyond the line of scrimmage? What difference does it make as long as the quarterback can complete the pass? The lack of rationale isn't as dumb as it appears. If the quarterback can run 10 yards then throw the ball from beyond the line, no defensive player could afford to tackle him, because he'd have to leave the man he's covering to get to the running quarterback. That man would then be open for a pass. Conceivably the offense could score on every play. And that would be boring because we wouldn't get to see any hard hitting, hear the sounds of the pads cracking, or watch the sneaky plays.

The quarterback does not need to be big, although it helps if he is tall and has big hands. In most teams the offensive and defensive line is well over six feet so, if the quarterback is tall, he will have a better view of the field. He should also be confident and possess good ball-handling skills so he can throw the ball accurately and hit his man on the dime. Most boys can throw a football. What separates the boys from the men is the quarterback's ability to throw the pass so the receiver can catch the pass while running full stride downfield. Cockiness does no good for a quarterback who throws only ducks (a football that wobbles and spins end over end rather than in a tight spiral) to a receiver who is in the wrong place.

INTERIOR LINEMEN

The interior linemen consist of the **center, two guards,** and **two tackles**.

The center positions himself in front of the quarterback. The center appears to have a weird fetish about letting some guy stick his hands underneath his rump while fans of all shapes and sizes watch.

Each play starts with the snap of the ball. The center's mission is to get the ball to the quarterback. The center will accomplish this by snapping the football to the quarterback. The snap of the ball means the center passes or hands the ball from between his legs to the quarterback. Prior to the snap, the quarterback yells out a series of numbers, words, or sounds, or any combination of these to his team members (10, blue, hut). On just the exact predetermined sequence, the center hikes the football. The snap count is intended to confuse the defense, so the defense does not know which number is going to set the offense in motion. The defense then doesn't know when to start their attack.

A lousy snap means the quarterback may not be able to get a good grip on the football, have enough time to execute the play, or throw a good pass, which might ultimately lead to an interception or even a fumble.

After the center snaps the ball, his job is to help protect the quarterback. The more time the quarterback has, the better chance he has to find the open man to whom to pass or hand the football.

In a shotgun or a single-wing formation, the quarterback does not reach underneath the center's rump for the ball. The center actually tosses the ball between his legs to the quarterback. This is not as easy as it looks. Try it sometime. Bend over and try to throw the ball from between your legs to someone who is standing about six feet behind you. And then imagine someone try to push you down or out of the way as soon as you have hiked the football.

The center should be big and fast. Although he does not have to be the biggest guy on the field, he should be quick. If the center is short and fat, it is hard for him to move around the defense. You do not want a little slug protecting the quarterback.

The guards are stationed on each side of the center. The guard's mission is to guard the quarterback by blocking and keeping the defenders away. Depending on the play, the guard may pass block or pull.

On a pass block, the guard tries to keep the defenders away by forming a pocket of players around the quarterback, protecting the quarterback, and allowing him more time to throw the ball.

Pulling moves the players from the strong side to a parallel position. Pulling is a deceptive movement in an attempt to move the defensive players from the strong side to the weak side. The strong side is where the majority of the offensive players are lined up. The guard runs in a horizontal movement, picking up the defender who is not covered.

Think of it this way. You (a guard) are in the market (the field of play). The market is giving away samples of chocolate cake (the football); as usual you have been on a diet for your entire life or what seems like your entire life. Unfortunately the line for the cake is two ladies deep on the left (weak side) and three ladies deep on the right (strong side). Rather than waiting in line you decide you are going to get that cake now. You run a diversionary tactic. You blurt out "Eight hours of free daycare, please see the store manager in Aisle 2B" (deceptive move). In a flash the two ladies on the weak side dash from the sample line to Aisle 2B. You have effectively moved to the head of the line for the yummy chocolate cake. This is a "pull." You have pulled the two ladies from the sample table (weak side) to Aisle 2B. You are now in a position to have the cake all to yourself.

The guard must be quick so he can adapt to the changing plays. A guard should be able to remember his assignments and be able to improvise when a play breaks down. He should be flexible and strong since he uses his entire body to block a defender. The guard should also love pain, since the next morning he is going to be one broken, hurting unit.

The tackles are positioned on each side of the guards. Their assignments are less strenuous than the guards. The tackles' main job is to protect the quarterback.

A blown protection can result in the quarterback getting sacked. Under pressure the quarterback may rush to get the pass off, resulting in an interception or an incomplete pass.

The tackle should be really big. In fact, the tackles are usually the biggest linemen. Since the tackles line up across from the defensive linemen, you can't have a wimpy tackle. If the offense has wimpy guys out in front, it is not going to be a pretty sight.

RECEIVERS

The **receivers** are going to be the speed demons of the team. The receiver's job is to get open, catch the football, run, and score a touchdown. The receiver does not want to drop the football (fumble), let someone else catch the ball (interception), have a defensive player rip the ball from his clutches (stripped), or not make the catch (incomplete pass).

Prior to a catch, the football cannot touch the field. If the ball first hits the ground, a shrewd player quickly falls on the ball and pretends he caught it. This is where acting classes pay off. However this is called "trapping" the ball, and officials will rule the pass incomplete.

The defender's job is to stop the receiver from catching or moving the ball. Therefore the receiver needs to be able to outrun the defender. Otherwise the roles could be reversed. The defender could end up catching the ball and the receiver would have to catch and tackle the defender before he does something stupid like score a touchdown.

Catching the football in the end zone is actually an art form in itself. Watch a receiver as he runs into the end zone. He keeps his eyes fixed on the ball overhead, makes the catch, keeps control of the ball, and at the same time keeps his feet in the end zone. This takes a lot of concentration, determination, and skill. Here is where the ballet classes paid off for these boys.

Depending on the play, a receiver can either be a **split end**, **tight end**, or **wide receiver**. On a long pass, these players are easy to identify, since in theory they are supposed to be the first players down the field to catch the football. The wide receivers should be able to jump from the line just like a bunny rabbit and sprint like a gazelle. If they are not fast enough to beat the defense down the field, then chances are they are playing in the wrong position. After all if the defense gets the ball before the receiver, well, you better find another receiver. What happened in this situation was the defense intercepted the ball and the offense got their butts chewed out.

The split end lines up several yards from the tackle or tight end. The split end's job is to catch the ball when thrown to him and run for the touchdown.

One of the quickest athletes on the field is the split end. The split ends' physical attributes, as the position title might imply, does not have anything to do with the condition of his hair. He is able to jump off the line and quickly move into his pass route position (similar to a bus route). If he is unable to beat the defense to the ball then a good defensive player will be all over him like bees on honey.

The tight end lines up next to the tackles. His mission varies depending on the play. In some situations the tight end may be required to block like a tackle or run downfield and wait for the football to be thrown to him. In this situation, his role is the same as that of a wide receiver.

The tight end is usually a well-rounded athlete because the variety of roles he is expected to play. The tight end does not need to have the tightest buns on the field. He should, however, have size and strength, though he does not need to be as big as the tackle. He must be quick enough to block the defensive end and fast enough to catch the football like a split end. The tight end is usually the slowest, biggest, and least graceful of the receivers.

The head of household, Mom, has many of the same attributes as the tight end. While preparing her normal gourmet dinner, Mom hears a faint scream from the rear bedroom, the sound of furniture hitting the closet doors, and not an unfamiliar sound. Her instincts take over and she runs a 4.8 40-yard dash to the back room. To no surprise, she finds that Chris has one of the neighborhood boys, Lonnie, pinned to the ground. The furniture is no longer in its original position. Barney (the dog) is yelping at the neighborhood boy; he doesn't quite understand Chris is the aggressor. Mom instinctively takes steps to resolve the situation.

She reacts quickly (explodes) with what she sees. She positions herself next to Lonnie (offensive player—tackle). Because she has both size and strength over these overzealous kids she quickly gets the situation under control. She then takes over the various roles of the tight end. She:

➢ Orders Chris to get off Lonnie (role of mother).

➢ Quickly checks Lonnie to make sure he has no broken bones, bumps, or open flesh wounds (role of nurse) and then accompanies him to the front door (role of butler).

➢ Demands that Chris move the furniture back to its original position (role of interior designer).

➢ Commands Barney to the backyard (role of dog trainer).

➢ Walks back to the kitchen to finish her gourmet dinner (role of chef).

Occasionally a receiver may have to act as a decoy, pulling a defensive back away from the football and toward the receiver. The quarterback can then attempt to do something underhanded, sneaky, or sly in an effort to move the ball downfield.

Let's go back to the market. Suppose your attempt at "pulling" the ladies from the sample table did not work. You still have one mission: Get that chocolate cake. So you decide to use your husband (receiver) as a decoy. Your husband stands at the back of the noodle aisle bare breasted and starts reciting lines from Cyrano DeBergerac. This distracts the other ladies away from your chocolate cake.

In certain situations, receivers may also be called upon to handle a wide range of assignments, including blocking the big defensive lineman or running with the ball. For just these reasons, the receiver should be quick, have good hands, and be smart.

Real football players love the physical aspects of the game, not just the glory. Consider the great Jerry Rice. He not only loves to score the touchdown but he also loves to kill the opponent. At least it appears that way.

RUNNING BACK

The **running backs** stand behind the quarterback. He can either be a **tailback, fullback,** or **halfback.** By watching the offensive formation you can determine what role the running back is playing.

The running back runs forward with the ball, not backwards as is implied in his name. His mission is to catch the pass or receive the hand-off from the quarterback and then run in for the touchdown. The running back is the focal point of any offense. A good offensive team must have a running and a passing game. This allows the team to mix up the plays so the defense has a harder time figuring what the offense will do. If you do not have good running backs, then you will not have a good running game.

A good running game requires size and speed. A good passing game requires the offense be positioned correctly on the defense. The offense must be at the right place at the right time while at the same time trying to confuse the defense so they can not read the play and mess it up for the offense.

The fullback lines up 3 yards behind the quarterback. The success of the fullback is key to the success of the offense. He sets up other runners with blocks or fakes. He provides the quarterback with pass protection. He runs the ball up the middle. He's routinely expected to pick up short gains. He is also expected to find a hole to run through or make a hole for someone else, pushing players to one side and allowing the ball carrier to run through the space or hole. He's usually considered the bull on the team; he uses brute force to advance the ball. Sometimes the fullback takes a fake handoff and challenges the defense to come and get him. See why football players are considered brainless? After all who in their right mind would challenge a 300-pound madman to come and get you?

The halfback lines up behind or to either side of the quarterback. The halfback is fast, elusive, and strong. On a running play, he carries the ball the majority of the time. Since this is the man who the team depends on to move the ball, you will not see the team's 90-pound weakling doing the job. The team weakling should be the water boy or the statistician.

In summary the offensive player positions:

MAIN POSITION TITLE:	SUB POSITION TITLE:
Quarterback	
Interior Lineman	Center, Guard, Tackle, and End.
Running Back	Halfback and Fullback.
Receiver	Split End, Tight End, and Wide Receiver.

CHAPTER 12

THE SWARMING BEES (Defense)

In most cases, the defense is overshadowed by the offense. If a team wins, the offense gets most of the glory, but if a team loses, the defense takes most of the heat. But anyone who knows anything about football knows that while "offense sells tickets, defense wins championships."

When playing defense, speed and quickness are more important than size and weight. Speed and quickness allow a player to hit, react, and move toward the ball.

Defensive football is simple: Tackle the ball carrier or bat the ball away from the opponent. One thing the defense cannot do is maim the opponent. This is not a game of gladiators, so spearing with the helmet, punching in the head with a fist, grabbing a facemask, kicking or tricking, or jumping onto a pile of players are considered poor sportsmanship. Doing any of the above will earn a team a 15-yard penalty. It could also result in ejection from the game and/or a personal fine for the player who gets caught.

In the first century the poet Manilius described gladiators and their profession by saying, "It would take a desperate and violent man to take on this career." The same could be said of the game of football. Football players are a special breed onto themselves—maybe not desperate but certainly violent.

The similarities between the gladiators and football players are striking. While both are a great source of public entertainment, thanks to technology, football can also be enjoyed by the private sector. The protective equipment worn by the gladiators has been modernized for the game of football. Shields, armor, headpieces, and knee plates are out and shoulder pads, knee pads, thigh pads, rib pads, hip pads, facemasks, and helmets are in. The weapons and artillery used in football are the actual plays and the various players' body parts. The arena has been renamed to add a little more class to this vicious sport, hence we have the field of play. Both are lucrative businesses for the promoters and the owners. Although when watching the gladiators, it was not uncommon to hear the crowds cheering for flogging and death of the opponent. You will not hear these barbaric outcries at a football game, but you will hear the crowd go wild when they see a good clean hit.

A defensive player is able to react and adjust quickly to the offense's formation. The defense knows where to line up to be the most effective. The more experienced defenders watch the offense and adjust to match the strengths of the offensive formation. If the defense does not make the necessary adjustments, the coach calls a time-out, pulls the player off the field, and tells him politely where the hell he should be.

The defense has the tougher job since they usually have to guess as to what the offense will do. That is why it is imperative that a good defense be able to read the play before it happens and adjust accordingly. Otherwise you have a defensive team playing catch-up. Getting behind the ball carrier is a mistake. To avoid this, the defense often moves or attacks at an angle. This allows the defense to get in front of the ball carrier before the offense can make quantum yardage or, worse yet, score.

Angling on a defensive play is similar to the actions of a defensive driver. You, the defensive driver (defensive player), attempt to get Fran to football practice (offensive player with the ball) without getting in an accident (blocked) or getting a ticket for speeding (illegal play). This means, for most of us, keeping our eyes open, so when that idiot driver (blocker) slams on his breaks for no apparent reason, you don't kiss his bumper. You may need to quickly swerve (angle) around the car to get to your destination (offensive player with the ball) in one piece.

A defensive player has the ability to read the play, stay with the play, and then, when it is time, kill members of the offensive team. If the defense moves the wrong way, it means the defense must figure out what went wrong and adjust, which all takes time. When it only takes seconds to move the ball, time is not a commodity the defense has.

Correctly reading the offense allows the defensive linemen a split second to figure out what the play is and/or what direction the offense is planning on moving the ball.

For example:

➤ If an offensive lineman starts running downfield, chances are the play is going to be a running play. Now all the defensive linemen have to figure out is which player has the ball, then kill the guy with the ball.

➤ If an offensive lineman moves to the right or to the left, the play is likely going to move in that direction. Although watch carefully that the offense does not attempt to trick the defense into going in the wrong direction. That is often called a misdirection play.

➤ If an offensive linemen starts backing up toward the quarterback, the play is likely going to be a pass play. The offensive linemen back up to protect and give the quarterback time to throw the ball. The linebackers watch the direction the quarterback throws the ball and then moves to cover the receiver in the area the ball is being thrown.

The attitudes of the defensive players will make or break the team. Defensive players like: (1) to hit, (2) to get hit, (3) to battle, (4) to be in control, and (5) to outlast the opponent. Other than that, they can be wimps.

The defense hits with enough brute force to knock the offensive player's head off, initiate the attack, control the opponents, avoid the block, find the player with the ball, and maim anyone who gets in the way. That's it.

The defensive player must not let the offensive player know he is a warm, sensitive marshmallow at heart. But instead they must portray a cold, calculating son of a bitch. To create this illusion, the defensive player uses not only strong body language but also does a lot of trash talking. The combination of these two strategies is an attempt to intimidate the offensive linemen.

DEFENSIVE POSITIONS AND RESPONSIBILITIES
INTERIOR LINEMAN

The defensive or interior linemen are the **noseguard** (player in the middle of the line), two **tackles** and two **ends**. They position themselves 1 yard behind the line of scrimmage. The linemen are (better be) in the middle of every hand-to-hand battle. The basic defensive stance involves lining up with the legs slightly apart and the arms dangling. Not because they are imitating the really hairier species but because the stance allows the defensive player to knock out his opponent with a blow from his hands, arms, and shoulders. The interior linemen stand in a three-point stance. When the interior linemen have both hands on the ground, this is a four-point stance. A "down lineman" is not depressed, nor is he down and out, nor is he down to earth. He is called a down lineman because he is either in the three-point stance or in a four-point stance.

The interior lineman's mission and key to success is his ability to control the line of scrimmage, which means they need to bigger and stronger than the defensive line. They must be able to react quickly in order to get to the line first and get to the ball carrier. He has no respect for the opponent's territory.

The **interior linemen** battle with and fight through the offensive blocks to get behind the offensive linemen. Getting past the offensive line and to the quarterback or his target means the defense has penetrated the offensive line. And not that kind of penetration either. Penetration, in football lingo, means getting past the line of scrimmage.

The **defensive linemen** must be able to read and understand the play. To accomplish this goal, most linemen commonly use three techniques:

➤ Read technique: The defensive lineman hits the offensive lineman with his forearm or hands. He then quickly moves to split the two offensive linemen out of his way so he can get to the football. The objective is to get past the line of scrimmage and to the quarterback before he can throw the ball.

➤ Slant technique: The defensive linemen line up across from the offensive linemen. The defensive lineman moves diagonally, pushing pass the opponent and into the open area to get to his target.

➤ Swim technique: The defensive linemen line up across from the offensive linemen. The defensive lineman then use his arms, as if swimming, to bat the opponent out of his way.

The interior lineman keeps the pressure on the offensive line. If he doesn't, he ends up getting pushed around and out of the play. When this happen, the interior lineman ends up wasting valuable time trying to figure out how to get back in the play. All this happens within a few seconds.

The **noseguard** is usually the leader of the pack on the defensive line. He is positioned directly opposite the offensive center; he is the center man on the defensive side. His main job is to stop the run, get the quarterback or get the ball carrier. The noseguard sees action from all sides. Once the ball is snapped, the center attempts to push the noseguard away from the quarterback so that the quarterback has plenty of space and time to get the football to a receiver. On the flip side, the noseguard attempts to push the center away so he can get to the quarterback. If the noseguard was unsuccessful in getting to the quarterback before he got rid of the ball, then the noseguard must get to and kill whoever has the ball.

The **defensive end** is positioned within 1 yard of the line of scrimmage and stands opposite of the offensive tackle. The defensive end's responsibility is to keep the ball and player inside, to prevent the player with the ball from moving to the outside of the defensive end. This is called containment. If the offensive player runs to the outside and down the line, chances are the defensive end blew his assignment.

Because the defensive end has to fend off a number of offensive linemen, he needs a strong upper body. In addition he should be quick, have speed, and be able to maintain body balance.

The two interior defensive linemen, regardless if they line up opposite the offensive guards or line up against the center, are still affectionately called defensive tackles. Because the defensive tackle must hold his ground, size is important. These guys are the anchors of the defensive team. They are responsible for sending the front wall flying across the line of scrimmage. They keep the blockers busy so the inside linebackers can set their sights on the football.

The **defensive tackle** should be able to penetrate (these guys really like to penetrate) the offensive line and break up the running and pass play. On a pass play, the tackle helps to break down the pocket and rush to sack the quarterback.

The **linebacker** lines up opposite the tight end or to the inside of them. They stand between 1 and 4 yards behind the line of scrimmage. His mission is to plug up (fill up) any holes the offensive linemen has made, theoretically stopping the offensive player from running through the hole with the ball. The linebackers are the meat and potatoes of any great defense. When the defensive lineman are not able to stop the offensive attack, then it is up to the linebackers.

The linebackers need to be strong. In fact, these guys should be the strongest guys on the field. Consider this: If the defensive linemen can not stop the offense, then you better have something stronger, bigger, and meaner to do the trick. In addition to strength, they must be able to move quickly and react instinctively to what is happening on the field. The linebacker should have good technique and be tough as nails, and mean as a bull. These guys must be strong enough to stop an opponent who is bearing down on them with a full head of steam. They must deliver a blow with a quick step and take a stand.

The **secondary linebackers** are stationed 2 to 8 yards behind the line of scrimmage. They line up opposite the wide receivers. The secondary linebackers are the guys who tackle the guy who has caught the pass or is attempting to catch the pass. For this reason, the secondary better be fast enough to catch the wide receiver.

To further confuse the novice football almost-fan, secondary linebackers are also called **defensive backs**. And if you didn't think that was confusing, they further break down the position to a **deep back**, **safety**, or **corner back**. Bottom line: The defensive backs are the last guys on the defensive side. If the offensive team can pass these guys, the touchdown is all theirs. You can see why the secondary linebackers must be strong and fast enough to stop the player who has slipped past the first line of defense.

When you see the quarterback throw the football to a receiver, watch the secondary linebacker run back, and cover the intended receiver while at the same time keep his eye on the ball, not the receiver. The secondary linebacker is looking for an interception, the ultimate glory.

In summary the defensive player position:

MAIN DEFENSIVE POSITION	SUB DEFENSIVE POSITION
Interior defensive lineman	Noseguard, Tackles, & Ends
Linebacker	None
Secondary Linebacker or Defensive backs	Deep back, Safeties, & Corner back

CHAPTER 13

SUICIDE MISSIONS (Special Teams)

Special teams are the teams used by coaches for specific situations to get specific results. These teams include kickoff, kickoff-return, all hands, punt, punt return team, and point after team.

Whether the team kicks or receives the ball dictates the type of players that take the field. The respective players line up in either the "attack" or "kill" formation. The "kill" formation is for players from the kickoff team, while the "attack" formation is for players from the receiving team.

The receiving team lines up in the "attack" formation and then attacks the barrage of meat that attempts to stop or block the ball carrier.

And you probably thought special teams were for players who were not good enough to start or play on offense or defense.

KICKOFF/KICKOFF-RETURN TEAM

On a kickoff, the kicker's strategy is to kick the ball deep into the opponent's end zone and away from the opponent's best returner. Members of this elite group of bad boys are capable of kicking the football as close to their end zone as possible and destroying any player trying to run the ball downfield.

Unless your team is receiving the football, you definitely do not want to see the person catching the ball return the ball for a touchdown.

The logic for both formations is quite simple. The kicker from the kickoff team boots the ball as close to his team's end zone as possible. The sequence of events is, the ball is kicked, and the kickoff-returner attempts to run downfield and as close to the their end zone as possible or even into the end zone for a touchdown. The kickoff return team charges downfield, killing any player or players who attempt to block, hit, or move the ball downfield. These players love to punish any player who has the audacity or courage to line up with the receiving team.

If a team does not have a good kicking team, then it has to rely on the offense to move the ball. Relying on one part of the team decreases the chances of moving the ball across the end zone. Even in the game of life, relying on one person when you have a two-man job minimizes the efficiency and effectiveness of the entire team.

A kicker only capable of kicking the ball a measly 10 yards means the defense must be that much stronger to stop the opposing offense.

The kickoff team runs onto the field to start the game, start the second half, after a touchdown, or after a field goal. You will never see a football player walk onto the field. This is part of the "I cannot wait to abuse and maim" philosophy. Also coaches hate to see players walking and taking a leisurely attitude. Players selected for the kicking team must like to hit and annihilate any player who comes trotting down the field. For this reason, you won't see a player who is intimidated at having a 300-pound animal foaming at the mouth charging at him. As most football players say, "football is 85 percent mental and 30 percent physical." Therefore coaches select their most aggressive players for the kicking team.

If the ball goes out of bounds before the kickoff-return team touches the ball, the kickoff-return team can either take possession of the ball where the ball goes out of bounds or 30 yards from the point of the original kickoff. College ball requires the kicking team kickoff again from 5 yards further back.

The player catching the ball is called either a safety or kick returner. His job is to catch the ball and run up the field without being tackled, without fumbling the ball, or without having the ball stripped. In fact it would be best if he could stop wasting everyone's time and just score the touchdown. But this would take the excitement out of the game. No contact, no hard hits, no delays of game—what are we thinking?

When a kickoff-returner catches the ball on the playing field, he can catch and then run with the ball, or he can opt for a "fair catch." Keep reading for the definition of a fair catch. The returner should always have control of the ball before he starts running. Otherwise he is likely to fumble, have the ball stripped, or just drop the ball. And then it doesn't matter how spectacular the catch was.

The kickoff-returner can signal a fair catch by waving one arm above his head. Do not confuse the fair catch signal with a player trying to rile the fans. Riling up the fans is done prior to the start of a play or after a play, but never during a play. If a player is trying to rile up the fans during the play, he belongs on the cheerleading squad. A kickoff-returner signals a fair catch when he does not have a chance of making a good run without being tackled or if he's afraid of being mangled and/or abused. Once a fair catch is signaled, the defensive players cannot attempt to tackle, touch, or even get in the way of the returner. If the defensive player does tackle, touch, or get in his way, it is a penalty. Once a fair catch is signaled and acknowledged by the official, the official places the football at the spot where the football was caught.

Mom invites a guest for dinner. The youngest sibling, Rob (kicker), can't stand the dinner guest, Mike, (best kick returner). Rob's mission (kicker) is to make the dinner experience as unpleasant as possible for Mike so he won't want to come back. He enlists the help of his three brothers (kickoff team). Accordingly, when Mike asks Rob for a freshly baked roll (attempts to catch the football), Fran does whatever it takes to keep the roll from Mike. Rob (kicker) grabs the roll (football), chucks (kicks) the roll over everyone's heads (ball caught on 1 yard line), and right smack in front of the drooling mouth of the family dog, Barney (third best kick returner).

Fran and Rob must stop Barney from dashing out of the room, hiding behind a tree, and eating the roll (scoring a touchdown).

At the dinner table, this may be inappropriate behavior. However in the vicious and violent world of football, this would have been a great maneuver since:

> ➣ Rob (kicker) did a great job of creating havoc at the table by throwing (kicking) the roll (football) to Barney (third best kick returner) instead of Mike (best kick returner).

> ➣ Mike (best kick returner) never got the roll (football).

> ➣ Rob and Fran where able to get Barney to release the roll (football) before Barney was able to high tail it behind the tree (touchdown).

Prior to the start of the game, with the help of the kickoff teams, the coach sets the tone for the rest of the game—show the opponents they are out for blood and guts. It seems silly, but these guys must prove they are the biggest, ugliest, and meanest.

Setting the tone of the game is not just important, it is imperative. As it breeds confidence in the players and motivates and gives the players a certain "high" to do what needs to be done. This is especially true when a team is inexperienced; the immature team may not be able to handle a team coming out strong and beating the crap out of them on the first play. They may emotionally feel defeated, like children who do not get their way, and sit and pout for hours.

In judging a good kick, watch to see:

➤ If the football is kicked deep into or even out of the end zone and into "Timbuktu" (that's similar to Never Never Land). When this happens, the official places the ball on the 20-yard line.

➤ If the kicker can kick the football really, really high so it hangs in the air for four to five seconds. A kicker worth his salt should be able to kick the ball at least 35 yards downfield. This also allows the kicking team time to get their butts downfield to minimize any gain on the return. While the kickoff-return team is waiting for the ball, to drop the kicking team is charging downfield to kill the kick returner.

Once the ball has dropped and a player catches the ball, then it is open hunting season on the kick returner.

ALL HANDS TEAM

The all hands team takes the field when the coaches have called for an onside kick. An onside kick is a team's last ditch effort to regain possession of the ball. The kicking team lines up to kick the ball as though it is going to be a regular kickoff. However the desperate coach pulls out all stops in an attempt to get the ball back. This is accomplished using the old "skipping and bouncing" technique. Instead of kicking the ball deep, they attempt to kick the ball so it skips and bounces, making it hard to catch. Once the ball has traveled at least 10 yards, the kicking team run like maniacs in an attempt to recover the ball before the receiving team does. The receiving team, however, can grab the ball as soon as they can get their mitts on it. Many couch potato quarterbacks forget that the receiving team does not have to wait for the ball to travel 10 yards. If the kicking team recovers the ball before it has traveled 10 yards, the receiving team gets the ball at the spot where the ball is recovered.

Now you can see why a coach selects players who are quick on their feet, who have good hands (not necessarily manicured), and who have the ability to hold onto the ball. For that matter, you can now appreciate why this team is called the "all hands team or the good hands people."

PUNT/PUNT-RETURN TEAM

On a fourth down situation, and only in a fourth down situation, the offense may opt to punt the ball rather than attempt to gain the first down. This is because the coach is not optimistic about the offense gaining the necessary yards for the next series of downs.

When the punting team is called into action, the punter runs onto the field and does his best to boot the ball as close to their end zone as possible. You can see why the ability to kick the ball deep into the punt-return team's end zone dramatically increases a team's chances of stopping the opposing offense. Moving the ball 55 yards for a touchdown is easier than moving the ball 75 yards for a touchdown.

Suppose the punter is really a frustrated basketball player and he screws up the kick. The ball travels a piddling 5 yards and begins to bounce.

If the punt-return team decides it is too risky to try to pick up the bouncing football, they can back away from the ball and let the ball die. In this case, the official places the ball where the ball stops rolling or goes out of bounds. The offense then takes over at that spot. If the ball takes a weird bounce and starts to go backwards, the punting team can touch the ball to stop the play. This is actually considered an illegal touch and the opposing offense gets the benefit of taking over where the punting team touched the ball. If, however, the punt-return team tries to pick up the ball that is bouncing all over the place and muffs it, then it is a live ball. Any team can recover it as a fumble. If this happens, train your binoculars on the punt-return team's coach and watch his histrionics.

POINT AFTER TEAM

The point after team attempts the point after (extra point) after the offense has scored the touchdown. In professional ball, the extra point is attempted from the 2-yard line. In college and high school, the extra point is attempted from the 3-yard line. With the kicker so close to the goal posts, it seems like a kicker should be able to make the extra point 100 percent of the time. However, the pressure of the situation, along with visions of huge hunks of meat charging at you, adds a certain element of difficulty to the kick.

If the punt after team messes up and misses the point after point, the ball is marked dead and the play is over.

Tony, chief chef (coach), uses family members (special teams) quite effectively for specific end results. Special kitchen teams might include table-setters, dishwasher crew, or table-cleaners. The requirements for each team may require Tony to match the specific qualifications with the specific results needed. After all Tony would not want to pick the midget of the group to put away the dishes.

But suppose Tony does select the midget to put the dishes away. Although this may not be the best selection, the midget will do his best to put the dishes away, even if it means he doesn't finish until right before the next meal. Bottom line: To have a successful team, it is imperative to select the right player for the right task.

CHAPTER 14

THE FLOCKING VOLLEY (Offensive Strategies)

Coaches use various strategies to outsmart their opponents. Prior to the game, in the heat of the battle, or at halftime, the coach will often use the old chalkboard method of communicating. To describe the formation to the players, the coach uses "O's" to describe the offensive player and "X's" for the defensive players. Coaches resort to this type of communication since quite often they cannot calmly find the words to articulate the consequences of what the players may or may not be doing.

This sophisticated system is called "chalk talk." Chalk talk is opposite of "pillow talk," although both are characterized by intimacy and secrecy. Chalk talk offers a hard, honest assessment of an event; pillow talk is usually a bunch of half-truths about how good the event was.

Pillow talk does not include illustrations, whereas chalk talk consists of charting how the play should have been executed and what the dumb player did or did not do. Perhaps if we used chalk talk in the bedroom, I could fall asleep as quickly as my husband does.

OFFENSIVE FORMATIONS

At the start of each play, each player on the field, regardless if they are on the offense or defense, will form a specific pattern on the field. This pattern is called a formation. The formation is what, it is hoped, will allow the coaches' strategies to be carried out.

There are a number of offensive formations, which make it easier to execute the plays. An offensive formation can take any form with a couple of exceptions:

➤ There must be at least seven players on the offensive line when the ball is snapped;

➤ Once the play is ready to roll or "set," the offensive players can not move, except for the "man in motion."

Following are the most commonly used formations:

➤ A tight formation calls for two tight ends (two are better than one!) and three running backs, creating an unbalanced line. This formation creates a simple power game—you just cram the football straight down the field. When the defense sees this type of formation, they know they are going to have to stop the run in order to stop the opponent from scoring.

➤ The second approach is to spread the players out with a number of wide receivers, maybe one running back, and no tight ends.

Formations used for the running game:

➤ Tight T formation: Also known as the T or basic T formation. The quarterback takes his customary position directly behind the center. The fullback lines up a few yards behind the quarterback, the two halfbacks station themselves to the outside of the fullback. Thus forming the letter "T."

➤ I formation: The running backs line up directly behind the quarterback, forming the letter "I." This formation is effective because the running backs are close in proximity to the quarterback to receive the hand-off. In this formation, the fullback may block for the halfback, also called a tailback.

➤ Power I formation: In this formation, the offense uses a lead blocker or two blockers to block the opponent at the point of attack. The blocker acts like a snowplow, clearing the route for the ball carrier. This is referred to as the power formation because the fullback blocks and leads the ball carrier through the hole.

➤ Double wing formation: The quarterback and fullback line up behind the center, forming a symmetrical line. The halfback and flanker line up behind and outside the end positions. Sometimes this formation is also called the one back formation.

➤ Full house backfield: The offensive players line up in a traditional T formation with three backs behind the quarterback and between the offensive tackles. This formation can be used as either a running or a passing play.

Formations used for passing plays:

➤ Spread formation: The running backs line up behind the line of scrimmage and just a little to the outside of the left and right tackles. With this formation, the running backs can jump off the line, allowing them to act as a fourth or fifth receiver.

➤ Shotgun formation: The quarterback stands all by himself, about 7 yards behind the line of scrimmage. The center has to hike the football all that way through the air, accurately and quickly. This formation allows the quarterback more time to scan the defense and find a free receiver.

➤ Wishbone formation: The wishbone formation used primarily by middle-division schools and high schools. Because of the danger to the quarterback and because it has a low percentage of passing effectiveness this formation, is rarely used by professional teams and division 1 schools.

➤ Flood formation: Three receivers line up to the outside on the same side of the field. This formation allows a team to "flood" the area with receivers. Also known as a "triple" since the offensive team uses three receivers, which hardly seems like a "flood" of receivers.

Choosing the right formation is the key to winning games. If the coach's vision works, he is a hero. If the formation is wrong for the situation, the coach is a lousy coach. When choosing the formation, a coach often combines two or three of his best offensive talents.

Rob, the winningest coach of the neighborhood, is masterful in selecting formations that frame the boy's talents. His talent consists of Barry, the running back and the fastest kid on the block. Lonnie, the fullback, is strong and can take down anything in his path. Mike, the quarterback, is a so-so quarterback. He has no passing game and he is okay at his running game.

Alrighty then—Rob can see that he has someone to run the ball, a good blocker, and a quarterback who probably better stick to handing the ball off. Rob's choices are easy. He can use the power I shotgun or a full house formation. Rob knows, these formations will work the best for these player's skills.

Successful sports programs use formations that allow for balance and consistency. The more times a play is run, the better a team will be. Vince Lombardi used the same formations over and over again, which allowed his team to become error free and gave his players confidence in what they were doing.

Also if you line up in the same formation, you can snooker the defense by running different plays out of that same formation.

OFFENSIVE PLAYS

Now that you can recognize the different offense formations, let's discuss the various plays you might see run within these formations:

- Draw play: The quarterback drops back, pretends he is going to pass, takes a few seconds, and instead hands the ball to the running back. With this delay, the offensive linemen are ready to block the defensive linemen who have penetrated (crossed) the line. This provides a hole for the running back to run through.

- Reverse/Double Reverse: A quarterback takes the snap, runs in one direction, and hands the ball to a running back running in the opposite direction. The running back (here's the tricky part) runs around the backside of the line, emerging on the other side of the field. This play normally works because the defensive players, who have been watching the quarterback, have a hard time changing direction to get to the running back. A double reverse is where the first reversing back hands off to yet another offensive player running in the same direction the quarterback has been running. You will hear the armchair quarterback yelling, "Double reverse!"

- Sweep: The running back takes a hand-off and then pulls the offensive linemen around one end of the line. The play, when run correctly, provides a wall of blockers around the runner, allowing the running time to get around the outside of the defense.

- Bomb: A long airborne pass to a receiver. This play has a low probability of success, since the timing between the quarterback and the receiver must be *perfecto*. If it works, the offensive team can gain 50 or more yards.

- Flea Flicker: A tricky play, run to fool the defense. The quarterback hands the ball off to a running back who runs toward the line as if it were a running play. When the running back gets the ball, here's the trick, the running back flicks the ball back to the quarterback who then passes it to a receiver downfield. This works if the defenders rush the line to tackle the runner, leaving receivers open behind them.

➤ Play action pass: The quarterback fakes a hand-off to a running back then drops back to pass. Offensive linemen join in the deception by acting as if they are blocking, drawing defenders who anticipate a running play up to the line. This leaves space in the defensive backfield for receivers to get open and catch passes.

➤ Screen play: A short blooper (pass) thrown over the heads of the onrushing defenders to a running back or receiver. The reason why it is called a screen play is because the blocker let their assignment (defensive player) run past them and then they set up a wall of blockers for the running back. The screen play is effective when the defenders have tried the blitz and failed.

➤ Option plays: An offensive player runs out of the pocket and toward the sidelines like a madman trying to find an open receiver to pass to. If he can't find anyone to pass to, he has the option of keeping the ball to himself to gain the necessary yards or tossing it to a halfback that is along side of him. The various options keep the defense off-balance because they do not know if the quarterback will run or pass until the last minute.

CHAPTER 15

THE SWARMING BEE MILITIA
(Defensive Strategies)

There are two factors that contribute to a win. The first is called the "point of exchange." The second is called "time of possession." The point of exchange is where the offense gives up the ball to the opponent. The time of possession is the number of minutes one team has the ball over his opponent. The team that cumulatively has the best field position and who has possession of the ball the longest usually wins.

Good field position rests on three factors: no fumbles, no interceptions, no turnovers. A fumble or an interception not only means possession of the ball for the opponent but usually means good field position too. If this happens, you can expect the coaches to verbally abuse the responsible player when he comes off the field.

Typically, unless the defense has recovered a fumble or made an interception, the offensive team should have possession of the ball. Possession is fundamental to winning. However possession only gives a team the opportunity. Which direction they turn the key dictates whether a team wins or loses. It really is quite rudimentary, my dear: If you don't have possession of the football, how are you going to get points on the board? If you finally get possession of the lumpy white potatoes but drop them on the floor (fumble) or lose them to one of the family members (interception), then it didn't do much good to have them in your possession.

The defense must stop the offense from moving the ball 3 1/2 yards per down. If this doesn't happen, simple mathematics shows that the offense will keep earning first downs. (3.5 yards times 4 attempts = 14 yards)

The defense wants to force ("force" is good football lingo and will definitely impress anyone listening) the offense into making errors. Good, solid execution will eliminate offensive errors. The more chances the offense has at moving the ball...well, it does not take a "Norman Einstein" (as Joe Theismann would say) to figure out they are going to move that ball unless they fumble or throw an interception.

In addition to forcing turnovers, the defense wants to exert enough pressure on the offense to break up the play. When this happens, the offense ends up scrambling to put a play together. The defense also wants to make the quarterback hurry on each play. This has a cumulative negative effect on the quarterback's decision-making and, it is hoped, will lead the quarterback to make a mistake. There is a balance of pressure the defense wants to maintain. If they bring too much pressure, the quarterback can step up in the pocket and let the defense go past him. Too little pressure can mean the offensive players swarm right by the defense.

The defense needs a plan that is well-coordinated. The plan must be designed to stop the offense cold in its tracks. Once the quarterback has received the play, it then becomes a game of matching strategies and tactics.

DEFENSIVE FORMATIONS

Following are four formations the defense is most likely to use, once they read what the tricky offense is attempting to run:

➤ 3–4 defense: Three defensive linemen line up on the line of scrimmage with four linebackers behind them; the four additional players are considered defensive backs. The four linebackers step forward to stop the running plays or back to cover receivers on passing plays. This formation is the most commonly used.

➤ 4–3 defense: Instead of three defensive linemen lining up on the line, the coach uses four defensive linemen and three linebackers behind them; the other four players are positioned as defensive backs. With the extra body on the line, he can help defend against the running play and help in creating a stronger pass, rushing defense. However if the offense throws the ball, the defense may be unable to quickly cover the receiver.

➤ Nickel or dime defense: A fifth defensive back, called the nickel back, replaces a linebacker on the field. A dime defense uses two nickel backs, a fifth and sixth defensive back, replacing the linebackers. Although this defense increases the pass coverage, it can also make the defense more vulnerable on running plays. The next time "the guys" are over for a big game and you can identify the defense, call out something like "The coach sure does like that nickel defense" and watch their heads spin right off their necks.

➤ Goal line defense: A defense places six or more players on the line in order to prevent the offense from running the ball into the end zone. Again this defense may leave the defenders vulnerable in a pass play situation.

DEFENSIVE PLAYS

Once the defense is set in their formation, just like the offense, the defense runs defensive plays to stop the offense. Following are six of the most common defensive plays:

➤ Zone defense: The secondary defenders are assigned to specific areas of the field rather than to individual receivers.

➤ Blitz coverage: Also called red dog or a dog coverage. Once the ball has been snapped, one or more of the linebackers or secondary linebackers charge across the line of scrimmage. If the blitz doesn't work, this leaves the defense vulnerable to various offensive plays. If it works, the payoff may be a turnover or a big loss for the offense.

➤ Man-to-man coverage: This is a difficult play to execute. Each defensive player is assigned a particular offensive player to cover. With this coverage, fewer passes are completed because the coverage is tighter.

➤ Prevent defense: Also called a victory defense. A defensive play used to prevent the long pass. The defensive backs line up deep, giving the receiver the opportunity to catch the short pass. In a prevent defense, some teams may use only three defensive linemen while other teams drop a fast defensive end into pass defense. When a team is in prevent defense a team is in deep zone coverage.

➤ Even defense: Defensive player is not aligned with the center, the defensive player is literally slightly off balance to the center. This play has nothing to do with the number of players, even or odd on the line of scrimmage.

➤ Gap defense: A defensive lineman is positioned in between the gap of the offensive lineman. The most common of the gap defenses is the "gap8," used for short yardage situations.

ENCROACHMENT
(Crossing into someone's bubble)

HOLDING
(Inappropriate bear-hug)

PERSONAL FOUL
(Saying things to hurt someone's feelings)

PASS INTERFERNCE
(Food tasting before it is served)

TOUCHDOWN
(The big one)

ILLEGAL PROCEDURES
(Taking trash out on wrong day)

CLIPPING
(Doing whatever it takes to control a child)

FACEMASK
(Grabbing onto a kids arm so they don't run away)

ROUGHING THE KICKER
(Picking on the littlest kid on the block)

ROUGHING THE PASSER
(Cheap shot on the main man)

1st DOWN
(My turn to go)

ILLEGAL BLOCK
(Throwing dish out when it was okay to eat)

DELAY OF GAME
(Stalling)

INTENTIONAL GROUNDING
(Not holding back your feelings)

LOSS OF DOWN
(To skip a turn)

ILLEGAL USE OF HANDS
(Not keeping hands to self)

TIMEOUT
(Same as what you tell a kid to do)

UNSPORTSMAN CONDUCT
(A dirty play)